Now and Then:
20th Century Change in America

James Leonard Delaney

© 2006 James Leonard Delaney

All Rights Reserved. No portion of the book may be reproduced in any fashion, either mechanically or electronically, without the express written permission of the author. Short excerpts may be used with the permission of the author or the publisher for the purpose of media reviews.

ISBN 0-9776207-2-7

Printed in the United States of America on acid-free paper

Layout and cover design by Sarah Nelson

Published by:

Westview Publishing Co., Inc.
PO Box 210183
Nashville, Tennessee 37221
www.westviewpublishing.com

To all citizens who hunger and thirst, yes search, for remnants of our once great united country; to all who persevere and sacrifice to preserve, protect and defend our culture, sovereignty and heritage, I dedicate this volume.

CONTENTS

INTRODUCTION vii
Part I: The Mind 1
1. Quo Vadis, USA
   (Whither Goest Thou, America?) 3
2. Getting the Word Out 8
3. Involvement 12
4. Where Have All the Snake Pits Gone? 23
5. Tyranny in the New World Order 27
6. Immortality Without Religion 30
7. Dogs and Kids Rule 33
8. Media Shame 37
9. Bilderberg 40
10. Avarice 42
11. Image 44
12. Fear 47
13. Guilt 51
14. Race 53
15. School Days 61
16. D-I-V-O-R-C-E 68
17. Religion and Politics 72

CONTENTS ...continued

Part II: The Body 75
18. Finger Food 77
19. Metabolism 80
20. Cooking, Anyone? 85
21. Hygiene 94
22. Soccer, USA 97

Photographs 99

Part III: The Earth 109
23. Farm Family 111
24. Scratch Biscuits on the River Bank 114
25. Adopt a Tarmac? 120
26. Flood 122
27. Aztlan 124
28. How Dense Can We Get? 127

Part IV: Toward the Unknown 131
29. Facts to Face 133

APPENDIXES 145
NOTES 151
GLOSSARY 152
BIBLIOGRAPHY 154
ACKNOWLEDGEMENTS 156

INTRODUCTION

Welcome to a log, an honest record of memory, past and present. Except for matters of national sustainability, it is un-opinionated, but with an objective purpose: to exhort the people to think critically, evaluate and act.

If entertaining, it was not meant to be, for it surfaces America's problems, yes, nightmares ignored by a plastic, mainstream, Orwellian media.

I was moved to write it because of last year's meeting with a fellow retiree. I had just finished a new revealing, five star biography of Alexander Hamilton and, being a widower, felt the need to discuss my "find" with SOMEBODY. Over coffee, I briefed my neighbor on extra-curricular, recent findings that led to Hamilton's fatal duel with Aaron Burr.

My neighbor stared at me blankly and replied: "Were they from here?"

This report is not a speech to convince, rather one to inform. Convincing requires pandering—a decadent form of entertainment which most Americans need for daily survival ("entertain me and I'll vote for you!"). It assumes that the virtue of individualism still burns brightly in drug free adult minds—the virtue that made America great.

This volume does not discuss the nuts and bolts of life's quality; yet, there are choices to make. If one's lifestyle is sessile like that of the oyster, he or she may be content to remain in the cocoon of security, existing on entertainment and news of cash-back bargains giving installed powers the right to manipulate their future at will.

However, if one is drug-free and active to the end of productiveness, you may want to reflect on past cherished values and needs, then compare, think, analyze and act. There are alternatives.

An appropriate title for this report would be "THEN AND NOW," but, alas, my hero of the plume, in both storytelling and pure prose, has already made it an entry in his vast repository… a late genius who may well be the critic's choice for both his centuries—Somerset Maugham

I. THE MIND

1. "Quo vadis, USA?"

(Whither goest thou, America?)

As a retired reporter, historian and public affairs officer, the interview was my forte. I love to interview Americans even when they are unaware the process is ongoing.

But for the one on one routine, I usually keep my hand in during a Wal Mart weekday session in the parking area. Armed with 20-30 frozen pizzas highly visible in a cooler, and a friend with a camcorder at my elbow, the procedure goes, thus:

"Good morning, sir/madame. If you have a free moment, I have a FREE pizza for you if you can answer three questions. O.K.? (I offer them my personal information card.) You may or may not appear on television, but your name is not required. Ready?" (Wal Mart customers and a FREE pizza; I get few refusals.)

"Question one. What is the population of the United States?" Average answer: "I don't know."

"Question two. Who are your three members of Congress?"

Average answer: "I don't know... or will give you wrong answers."

"Question three. When is the next NASCAR event?

Average answer: "A week from Saturday and I'll be there!"

When I tell this story from behind a lectern at luncheon meetings of Lions, Rotarians or Civitans, everyone laughs... and why not? Americans exist for entertainment. It's the Orwellian way.

But under the heading of common sense, the "dumbing down" is sadly tragic—once able and proud Americans settling back and giving "Big Brother" (Corporate America) a Carte Blanche to pursue its control and avarice at their expense.

A first magnitude example of this injustice is the ongoing chaos and relief following Hurricane Katrina when it came ashore at New Orleans in September, 2005. The populace, apparently, with all scientific data available to them as Katrina approached, elected to place their trust in Uncle Sugar and God by staying put.

In light of the misery that followed, Monday morning quarterbacking can be cruel, but for thinking Americans, points, outside biased media, have to be made.

Point one: How much of the scientific data was used by qualified/repeat/qualified people (as opposed to political appointees)? This responsibility includes levee inspection before and during the hurricane season, June through October.

Point two: Standing on their "civil rights." The populace as a whole refused to leave. But the governor, armed with proper statutes, has the power, backed up by the military, to ORDER evacuation. State Federal

Emergency Management Agency personnel, before the category four storm hit, had the option of marshaling hundreds of busses from surrounding states to carry evacuees inland. Trains were an overlooked resource.

Point three: The abject, welfare poverty in the city was bared for the rest of the nation to see. But this is not to single out New Orleans; dozens of other comparable cities share a third world status of doled out money and socialized medicine—all a product of Corporate America's plan for globalization (see chapter 8. Media Shame). If every head of household had occupied a meaningful job, the "tie" between city and citizen would have been dissolved long before tragedy struck.

Point four: some stricken residents, in their misery, even fired upon overflying rescue helicopters. This is not to say that guns are bad, but that rampant population density is. Population density, the number of bodies/occupants/residents/Homo sapiens per hectare, acre, square mile or unit volume affects us HERE (I touch my head/brain) and HERE (I touch my heart/metabolism). In times of stress, do-gooders become criminals; the young react to drama they've seen on television, etc.

Statistics one will not see in the media: The current U.S. Population is 300 million, soon to be 500 million if current immigration policies remain. Immigration, both legal and illegal, is the prime mover. Consider world population. Our incubator, countries between the Tropics of Cancer and Capricorn, is the main generator.

Women of child bearing years ovulate longer and produce more gravid eggs (ova) than their counterparts in more northern and southern latitudes—not a relevant statistic until major sponsors of the United Nations practically wiped out infant mortality. Today it's relevant.

It's natural for families everywhere to seek a better life. They come here unprepared, having heard of America's "Great Society" where anything is possible—anything goes.

President Vincente Fox (President of Mexico) maintains he has 20 million illegal aliens awash within our borders. The Administration, like the one before it, speaks favorably of our porous southern border and recommends periodic amnesties.

Florida appears to be the California of the 1950s—filling rapidly like pouring water into the condom shaped State it is. As global warming (partly, a function of world population) produces more hurricanes per season, the prospect of city misery above and beyond that of New Orleans looms high.

Since record keeping, the greatest hurricane disaster to strike the United States occurred on September 8, 1900. Thousands of non-residents had gone to Galveston (Island), TX, to escape the heat and enjoy the resort. Before the days of radar, satellites, yes, even radio communication and the automobile, five to six thousand people died or disappeared under the storm surge. The toll could have been GREATER but for the word from recently landed veteran fishermen that a surge was coming where the "sea got up on its hind legs and came ashore." If the people were drugged, it was from too much booze only, for many took action and evacuated across the causeways by horse, wagon or foot to higher ground. Finis to a story where humankind THOUGHT AND REACTED. [1]

But, in early 2005, we reacted WITHOUT THOUGHT when Terri Schiavo's name became a household word. Suffering from brain damage, kept alive by tube feeding, her husband and other family members suddenly elected to terminate food.

Her doctors advised that a prognosis for her recovery was negative. What followed was a shameful televised fiasco.

Terri was a young woman. Her "smiling" gape, characteristic of her affliction, told a layman world that she was "in touch," recognized people and enjoyed life—an impression which a cruel and inhuman press failed to correct.

Millions followed the slanted story; demonstrations to "keep Terri alive" appeared in Washington. On March 19, a Congress under pressure passed special legislation to resume her feeding.

A tabloid media was the victor, and family liberties, common and unpublicized in the 1940s and 50s perished, perhaps forever.[*]

---

[*] Having matured in an assisted living and nursing home environment, I witnessed many of these terminations which involved and concerned the family, attending physician and nursing home administrator ONLY.

2. Getting the Word Out

Following the Civil War, the newspaper trade exploded as printing presses matured and political bosses started their own scandal sheets to shape public opinion. 20th Century newspapers were a friend: They taught legal immigrants English, served as insulation under one's coat when Chicago-like winds were icy and even used by some as wallpaper.

Enter the amplitude modulated radio. Even before all households got electricity, a small crystal or battery powered radio kept Americans informed. My aunt, as a recent bride, praised the new wonder: "Programming was great and commercials few. When penned up because of weather, we were told what was going on and never bored." Sales of Atwater Kent, Philco, Zenith, and other floor and table models soared.

The telling of what was going on was the job of no-nonsense men of CBS, NBC, and Mutual: "Good evening, this is Elmer Davis with the news." A loud, well modulated voice spit out the down and dirty facts. If a station sugar coated a story, it was attacked by editorials from others. Politicians shunned the microphone unless reading a prepared statement.

Radio, truly began as a public service. But it didn't take power oriented owners long to realize their potential to control and influence while enlarging the lucrative business of broadcasting. Even newspaper moguls like William Randolph Hearst bought into it. Still, radio remained as clear, honest dispensation of the news—a format that could be understood by all.

World War II and technological advance produced a need for the foreign correspondent. What American, my age, can forget Edward R. Murrow's unique "This is London" leadoff? After the war, Ed and CBS's Fred Friendly made sweeping changes in radio that enabled Murrow and the network to make a successful transition to television in the 1950's.

By 1955, every American household had, or had access to, "the hooded cobra." Movie houses closed and TV dinners, before the fast food era, were the rule. Another rule, pushed by the blossoming industry, was "give 'em what they want," which meant, sometime squalid, entertainment in all genres—including news.

My thrust here is not to judge television entertainment's evolution. It's a broad spectrum, and my experience is in broadcasting, and psychology—not acting, producing and directing.

When television sprouted color, the networks likened themselves to Hollywood. No one in the towered headquarters complained that Dave Garroway or Robert Q. Lewis wore glasses, but fretting public relations personnel, paid to improve Neilson ratings, introduced a syndrome that remains bottom line today.

Over the years, I've labeled it a T-H-E syndrome that MUST be embraced by all news anchor hirelings. T-H-E means that one can not face the television public unless TEETH / HAIR / EYES are surgically corrected. Never mind diction, voice or clarity. Superficial cosmetics come first. Intelligibility is down the priorities list somewhere.

Today, young female anchor personnel raised in front of a television set are the worst offenders. They speak in a rhinoid tattoo[*] that only their contemporaries understand… and they truly are not responsible for this cultural shortfall that makes a mostly male audience ask: "What did she say?"

What is this sound under discussion? You have only to go to public television during early morning hours, or to weekend morning kid shows for a sample. The target audience remains the captive tot, ages one through four, ingesting all these abnormal voices produced by big business adults. Girls, because of hormonal and physiological differences, are more likely to develop and carry these sounds into adulthood. Boys, too, today are known to have their voices, even after puberty, remain on a higher frequency.

Remember the Bee-Gees, men in their thirties who were the musical darlings of our disco craze? They worked hard to perfect a sound of preteen girls; their universal popularity became a contributing factor. Add to that a culture rich in clipped speech and mumbling (diction and speech have disappeared from secondary school curricula), expose vulnerable children, ages 1-4, to it and you have part of the story of why it's so difficult to

---

[*] Sounds made by the vocal cords are forced out in the skull's rhinoid (nasal) area and controlled by abnormal use of tongue and palate…. as opposed to relaxed use of lungs and diaphragm.

get news you can use from the many modern television networks.

There is no point in documenting the media's fall from grace; the story is available elsewhere.* Retiring television anchor people allude to immortality without religion—which is getting to be the union card for Boomers. When newspapers, once staffed by Pulitzer Prize winners, embraced checkout lane tabloidism, television followed.

Crusaders of the 1970's that exposed Watergate lies and subterfuge have been replaced by robots that serve Corporate America's need for cheap labor through legislation like NAFTA, FTAA and CAFTA.

To that end, news writers and editors work in terms of checks and balances before air time with the eternal question: "How can we serve all interests concerned and still slant this?"

---

* See Bernard Goldberg's 2004 bestseller, BIAS.

3. Involvement

*"Goodness, after all, is the greatest force in the world
...and he has it!"
(Somerset Maugham describing
Lawrence Darrell in The Razor's Edge.)*

At age six, we lived quite near my grandfather who began to make almost daily inputs to my life. He quickly became an icon of the first magnitude.

During summer Saturday mornings, we usually walked a mile or so to his favorite fishing spot: The base of a powerhouse where effluent water from generator penstocks mixed with a river at right angles. At that point, fish food chains were mixing in the turbulent, highly oxygenated water and, for the fisherman, anything was possible.

We usually had the site to ourselves, for the county was still rural and Saturday was just another day for chores or laying in supplies.

About a quarter mile from the house we crossed the paved highway carrying a tied bale of four cane poles, lunch in a galvanized minnow bucket, a small tackle box and full canteen. Under a huge roadside oak sat a black (your only color choice) 1933 Ford sedan where two men supported another, obviously in great pain.

A fourth man was ripping his right trouser leg above the knee to expose a nasty wound: a four-inch section of the calf muscle (gastrocnemius) had been severed and was dangling.

Grandfather put down his fishing poles and commanded me to stay where I was.

"See here!" He spoke with a booming voice. "What are you doing to this man? What is going on? Are you drunk?"

The fourth man who appeared to be the only sober member spoke up, "We're his friends. About daylight, he got into a knife fight at this roadhouse (he named a county) and we beat it south before the cops came. We don't want no trouble; we stopped here to let him vomit." The victim had ripped off his shirt, exposing multiple non-lethal cuts.

"This man needs medical attention—now," grandfather continued. "Doctor Mooney is down this road about 500 yards, stone house on the right, you'll see his shingle. Tell him Delaney sent you. Now get this man home and ask God to forgive you for the sin that got him cut up in the first place!"

We continued on to the power house and had good luck, but grandfather didn't mention the four men in the Ford until we got back home, cleaned the fish and sat down to supper. He then briefed my grandmother, treating the incident as routine among the many in his life as a man of the cloth.

And indeed it was. That same summer, over my mother's objection, he took me on a quest I'll never forget. It was late afternoon when one of Henry Ford's late T models pulled up to Grandfather between his corn field and the house. A man in a slouch hat and overalls got out. I could see they knew each other, but there were no smiles. The man did all the talking, pleading his case which I could not make out. Grandfather remained pensive, looking down and nodding to his caller.

Back at the house, he grabbed my hand and briefed my grandmother: "I have to go with Mr. Jones[*] and I want to take Leonard with me. Don't worry, I'll leave him with Mrs. Jones and she'll feed him. I want him to know this family and learn about life. This is important. Mr. Jones is a member of our church and he needs me tonight. You probably know the facts already, but I'll fill you in later."

With that, my grandmother sighed and assented as if she had heard the "briefing" a hundred times. Grandfather put on his dark jacket and a felt hat, grabbed a fountain pen and his Bible and we were off.

Before leaving, we charged the T model's radiator with fresh water and it started without complaint. It chugged and smoked along at 20 miles per hour over an unpaved road that still showed wagon ruts. I was enjoying the ride, but not a word passed between the two adults.

An orange sun was setting under a cloudless sky as we pulled up to what I thought to be a final destination. A tall, gaunt middle aged woman who proved to be Mrs.

---

[*] To insure privacy, "Jones" is a pseudonym.

Jones greeted grandfather without cordiality, thanked him for coming and offered him a dipper of water from the front yard well which he took. She put her hand on my shoulder, guessed my age correctly and offered me the same.

Leaving me and the house cat on the porch, the three of them huddled near the Ford. Mrs. Jones seemed to be holding back tears as the Ford started and she watched it disappear around a turn in the wooded road.

To me, the house was strange. It was solid, built of oak, but you could see the Jones family was not the first to live here. The floors and porch timbers were well worn and appeared to be clean enough to eat from. It had a southern exposure, sitting against a ridge of oak-hickory that ran east and west—a good watershed for springs which fed he front yard well.

The house with a windowed attic sat on unmortared tiers of native (Cretaceous) limestone. Between the 2 foot high tiers on the north and west sides, additional rock slabs had been fitted as a winter wind barrier. Near the back door, a dugout under the house served as a root cellar: it was covered by watertight slanting doors similar to those of Great Plains storm cellars.

The outhouse had been built farther out in an area of deep soil and clay to permit absorption and assimilation. Still farther from the house, three young of the year hogs roamed a pen ready for late fall slaughter. Near a smoke house, the tools were ready: A large, black, cast iron kettle (soap making size), a well used cross section from a large tree to serve as butcher block and a 10 foot wooden tripod lashed at the top for hoisting the animals. Split firewood was stacked everywhere.

Mrs. Jones was an archetype of the rural period. As I reminisce, her image would today overjoy a Hollywood director casting such films as HOW THE WEST WAS WON. Her clean face was lined and her hair, streaked with gray and done up in a bun, was quite long.

"I'll fix your dinner," she announced, lighting a kerosene ("coal oil.") lamp. Coals in the huge cast iron stove still glowed, so she added kindling and brought the fire to life long enough to heat a huge ham slice in a cast iron skillet. To this she added a mound of turnip greens from a pot sitting on a cold back burner. A piece of day old bread completed my menu, and I ate with relish there in the kitchen, happy as a clam. Room temperature butter was abundant.

"We eat our ham cold in the summer, but I want you to have something hot before you sleep. It may be a long night. They've gone to see my husband's brother: He's the one who needs to see preacher Delaney." I asked no questions about where and why.

She stood, hand on hips, studying the floor as if planning the next day's events. Her unstained, threadbare dress was about six inches off the floor revealing leather shoes that could have been made for either sex. One was laced with a cotton cord, the other, a leather boot lace. The homemade apron was a permanent part of her costume.

Above a makeshift sink vented to the outside, hung a hemmed towel made from a cotton flour sack. The chair on which I sat had a much used cane bottom.* Similar chairs plus hand crafted tables and one double bed made up the house's furniture. Two galvanized tubs, one large enough for bathing, plus a copper boiler adorned the kitchen floor.

The house had been built around a chimney and fireplace of native limestone which provided basic winter heat. Its broad expanse which had burned endless cords of oak, hickory, and maple over a hundred years added still another dimension to the potpourri of odors, aromas, smells which entranced me.

Mrs. Jones transferred the oil lamp to the main room where we talked about my schooling and progress, mentioning a school, "a mile down the road" where her children had attended. Its schoolmaster, a veteran of 20 years, still ruled with "hickory stick, peach tree switch, or whatever was necessary."

She gave me a year old copy of the Saturday Evening Post, turned the lamp higher, sharpened a pencil, and then began to write "a letter to her daughter" in a neighboring state. We passed an hour in silence. She addressed her envelope, and then walked out into the darkness to "check the hen house."

---

* Footnote: During the 1920s and the Depression which followed, most counties of eastern states had small businesses which sustained local needs. Timber was abundant. Shops that turned out brooms, implement handles, cane bottom chairs and tables were everywhere. Profit, usually, was not an objective, and bartering occurred: A customer could bring in several dozen eggs and two smoked bacon sides and go home with his needs satisfied. Too, the ability to "bottom" a chair with split cane was a talent in need and sought out until around 1970.

Curious, I forgot the "Post" long enough to inspect the two west rooms. One had a narrow straight staircase, which led to the attic. The other held a modest double bed and a trunk, supplemented by a wall shelf with comb and broken mirror. These were winter sleeping quarters for the couple, for the outside walls were papered and insulated with newsprint. Some top layers were coming undone; it was time to reattach or add more with a simple flour and water paste—quite strong and efficient enough to keep our newspaper kites aloft in March winds. On one unpapered wall of the main bedroom hung a large black and white, framed picture of Franklin Delano Roosevelt.

Seeing that my eyelids were heavy, Mrs. Jones let me go outside to urinate in the dark while she laid quilt pallet and pillow for me by the unlit fireplace. She turned my lamp down low and lit another for herself. She said good night with: "Don't forget to say your prayers."

I slept the sleep of youth with a full tummy. Even sunrise and arrival of the noisy Model T failed to rouse me. Next thing I knew, grandfather was bending over me, stroking my hair: "Get up, boy, time to go home." I sprang up, stuffed in my shirt tail, went to the kitchen and poured water to wash my face.

For the first time during our trip, all three adults were smiling and sounding less grim. Mrs. Jones shed tears and hugged her husband. She offered grandfather a whole ham from the smoke house, which he refused. He held my hand while he spoke a brief prayer to our host and hostess and we were off.

On the trip back, grandfather and Mr. Jones smiled and chatted normally. He praised his brother they had spent the night with and used terminology which escaped me. The departing prayer had offered no clue. After all, I was only was into kite flying, fishing, and the rigors of school. Was there anything more to life?

Back home, grandfather brought my grandmother and me up to speed on his comforts while away: His hostess had killed a chicken and prepared a meal worthy of the governor. About midnight, he went to bed and slept until dawn. His face now showed stubble which embarrassed him, so he disappeared to remove it.

As to his mission, I wasn't included on the subsequent discussions which ensued. Only years later, when age bred secularism and puberty, was I fully "briefed" by my grandfather.

On that cloudless, summer day when Mr. Jones caught grandfather in the yard, his urgent, hand wringing message was: "Preacher we need your help. THERE'S GONNA BE A KILLIN' AND ONLY YOU CAN STOP IT!"

It seems that Mr. Jones' brother, a member of no church, had taken a local girl to be his wife—with no ring involved, they were "bespoken." But as luck would have it, she was a jezebel, playing the brother against his life long best friend for mostly entertainment. She was short of being marriage material and everyone knew it but the brother.

Insanely jealous, the brother caught "best friend" and jezebel in a compromising position and vowed vengeance. Too poor to own a handgun, he borrowed one from a WW I veteran in the next county, claiming a .45 slug in the brain of a hog was more humane than the ax. He drank and sat with the fully loaded weapon, asking himself: "Should I kill just him or both?" While working himself up to the act, no one dared go near him.

This then, was grandfather's mission: To approach the brother, reason with him and disarm the situation. The brother had refused to come to church; everyone labeled him as "no good."

Grandfather couldn't accept that condemnation. He knew that if a person was healthy (sane) he or she would accept logical doctrine or suggestions if they had nothing to lose and much to gain.

Arriving at his second destination that evening, he greeted his hostess, the brother's sister, and asked to be left alone with the tormented, potential killer. Closing the door behind him, grandfather removed his hat and coat advanced toward the brother, holding his thick bible over the heart in case insanity WAS present.

Grandfather was no stranger to violence and death, having served in the Philippines during the War with Spain. He had killed many Morros and the guilt that followed during the new centenary was partly responsible for his enrolling in a subsidiary of Brown University and becoming a minister.

The brother, one on one with his visitor, did not brandish his weapon. Instead, he let grandfather sit opposite him and talk quietly, not about the problem, but about the weather, when he had eaten and slept last. In ten minutes time, they were talking about guns and hunting. Grandfather reached over took the model 1911, .45 Colt automatic, removed the full clip and quickly field stripped it before the brother's eyes, rendering it useless.

Leaving the scattered parts on a bench, grandfather suggested a short walk around the house and up and down the road. With the inside lit lamps providing orientation, what followed next, out of family earshot, was a brief one on one sermon on the value of human life, yours, mine, the enemy's—the good, bad, and the ugly.

Thirty minutes later, they were on the back porch sharing a cup of hot soup. Grandfather talked about the girl friend, but didn't judge her. He assured there had been no coition between her and his life long friend. "You don't want to kill your best friend, you want to forgive him—AND her." They prayed aloud while touching; it seemed to be a new and pleasant experience for the would-be murderer. The sister interrupted long enough to serve supper on the porch. By ten p.m., the brother, shoes off, was snoring on an inside cot.

Came the dawn, he haltingly attempted an apology which grandfather shrugged off while embracing him. "This is a fine day; remember it!" Before grandfather left, the sister drew him aside and reported: "He knew about your faith and background in the war and all, but thought you would have no time to come and be with him." My grandfather always insisted he had no choice in these matters.

Today, this kind of "hands on" assistance is rare because it requires a trait our youth is taught to ignore (dare, I say it?)—responsibility... which is really a spin off of humankind's three guiding ethics: work, family and religion?

Recently, a night grudge fight occurred in a rear motel parking lot, the location doesn't matter, for it was captured on security videotape and broadcast nationally for the bizarre entertainment it offered.

Without knives or other weapons, two men fought to the death while three husky men, along with women and children watched. None of the onlookers reached for a cell phone, eventually, the larger man killed his opponent, inflicting head injuries. The management, at long last, called the police.

Later, the CSI force, through motel records, talked to the young, healthy witnesses who, collectively, could have prevented murder. They were asked why they failed to intervene. To a man, their answers equated to they "didn't want to get involved." [Note – see chapter 12 dealing with Fear]

4. Where Have All the Snake Pits Gone?

America's industrial might, long before the Second World War, hastened its contrived destiny. Even then, Corporate America became the traffic director, filling its labor requirement from rural ranks, often before the individual's psyche was ready to be uprooted.

This was an era long before avarice afflicted the Boards of Directors. Demands by labor were few. Modest pensions and a gold watch were the rule. Moving jobs abroad was 3-4 generations down the pike.

Foreign customers—today known as industrialized nations—had the ability to pay, and American three shift towns were born. In 1970, a partial roster of cities and their reason for being looked like this.

Portland, ME and Green Bay, WI – paper

Pittsburgh, PA and Seattle, WA – steel

Baltimore, MD and Phoenix, AZ – electrical machinery

Des Moines, IA – farm machinery

Houston, Beaumont, Odessa, and Midland, TX – oil, chemicals

Chattanooga, TN – textiles

Charleston, WV – chemicals

Computers and robots, which don't need to sleep, rest and relax, were non-existent, so a corps of "night people" appeared. Expensive manufacturing equipment had no time to rust, and the general manager (today's CEO) who kept it going twenty-four, seven got promoted.[2]

A working family became vagabonds. Kids were uprooted from schools almost annually. Social ties were broken and, by the 1960s, we had become a nation of stressed-out strangers, then referring to our homes as "split-level traps" where housewives often took refuge in a closet rather than answer the front door.

Treating veterans, who couldn't cope during and after WW II, fostered a great many stories about mental health, often written by psychiatrists or clinical psychologists. Indeed, the role of the state authorized and funded hospital has been preserved in book and film, revealing all its life-giving accomplishments, as well as shortfalls.*

As "public health in a free society" became an issue, the states responded with state-of-the-art medicine and technology, often using methods which today would be labeled "human rights" violations. In light of their restricted budgets, while dealing with an ever-increasing population, the personnel of these early institutions are to be commended.

Because the mission of these hospitals was little understood by former inmates or patient relatives, they

---

*Mary Jane Ward's powerful 1945 novel based on her medical and psychoanalytical experiences, THE SNAKE PIT, won accolades from the press and the medical profession. Two years later, 20th Century Fox made it into an award winning film.

were often called SNAKE PITS. True, they treated hereditary insanity, but too often the mind is affected by unsafe industrial and municipal practices. In the early 20th century, preventative measures (job safety) to protect the worker often went begging.

For example, little was known about ability of the human brain to withstand exposure to certain toxicants. Lead and natural gas, for example. Respirators and toxicant monitors were in their infancy and expensive. It follows, then, that businesses, to keep prices of their products down, would resist acquiring these devices. Profit, as today, but with a lesser ferocity, was the bottom line.

A brain-damaged employee, in his melancholia, was usually doomed to sit in the state institution until relieved by an early death. Since all human metabolisms differ, large businesses usually carried insurance policies on employees who worked in jeopardy, and also made tax-deductible contributions to the state hospital fund.

My research and exposure to "abnormal psychology" in the early 1950s introduced me to an expected number of catatonics and schizophrenics per 100,000 population. But the two surprising maladies committed to state institutions were acute narcissism and "flight into fantasy". Both are well examined in the Ward book cited.

Today, most state hospitals of the period, three generations old and built like fortresses, are alive and well. Their mission fits society's dilemma—the treatment of non-violent drug addicts. All residents are "trusties", and few vacancies exist.

Narcissism and "flight into fantasy" are no longer addressed by the mental health staff... BOTH MALADIES ARE NOW ACCEPTED AND PRACTICED ELEMENTS OF AMERICAN LIFE STYLE!

5. Tyranny in the New World Order

In a scenario of burgeoning population density (bodies per square mile) and failing budgets, America tends to abandon its heritage* and court mediocrity. Here's an example of how that abandonment has affected our judiciary.

Since the time of the Island of Manhattan's survey dividing it into residential plats, colonists and Americans have fiercely defended their turf from invasion and intrusion. If a neighbor's chicken flew over the fence and laid waste your garden, you simply wrung its neck and returned both parts to the neighbor's plat. The courts guaranteed your right to do this.

Welcome to the New World Order! The story you are about to read is true. To protect the evil, no names are used.

The players: The accused and abused we shall label "Old Guard." Retired and solvent, she was born when the family, religious, and work ethics were strong. Recently widowed (her late husband remains an icon in his profession), she contributes annually to many worthy causes. She panders NOT.

---

* Today, one cannot get an American History degree from our 51 major universities.

THE MIND

Which brings us to player two... who requires pandering—from the Government and other neighbors. Raising her children on a diet of Ben Spock, it put her elder in prison and gave the younger Carte Blanche to break neighbor's expensive windows with well-placed missiles. The husband has no opinion, simply taking and executing orders from a wife we shall call "Earned Income."

In 2003, Americans spent eight and one-half BILLION dollars on their pets. Earned Income fits the mold with a variety of pets which roam the neighborhood. Enter the conflict between the two archetypes...

Tired of Earned Income's pets decorating her lawn (and indeed between the toes while retrieving a newspaper), Old Guard fired a round of "dust shot" from a hand gun to discourage the animal while caught in the act. The pet was scared, not injured.

America's paranoia with the second amendment is decadent. Within minutes, local police responded to Earned Income's 911 call that a madwoman was running loose with a gun.

Old Guard was arrested and booked on multiple counts. In the fingerprinting process, a 300 pound police person "seemed to delight" in inflicting pain on the suspect's arthritic hands. (shades of national socialist Germany, 1933).

Aglow with her newly found power, Earned Income marshaled a dozen locals to help get rid of the "madwoman" in their midst. The group included a couple of Old Guard's "friends" of many years; they all displayed unified hate at the first hearing. Awash in the neighborhood of silence and intimidation, she moved from her home of 35 years.

This New World Order story*—An indictment of the present judicial system—has an epilogue our biased Orwellian media sits on. Point one: Non-citizen judges sit or have sat on benches of Southwestern States. Point two: Lip reading training is now part of curricula for new employees, Department of Justice. Comments discerned from a distance with binoculars may be used against you in a court of law. Did you say something about your Constitutional (first and second amendment) rights?

---

* The story smacks of Ayn Rand's 1946 novel, THE FOUNTAINHEAD, made into a Warner Brothers movie with Gary Cooper and Pat Neal. Set in America, it predicted a world where the gifted individual had no chance against a mediocre, Big Brother collective.

6. Immortality without Religion

"He who believeth in me, though he were dead, yet shall he live."

John 11:25

The above is attributed to Jesus after he brought Lazrus living from his tomb were he had been decomposing for four days.

I remember the story well from Vacation Bible School, a church program designed to occupy the time of preteens and compete with the likes of baseball, fishing and visiting grandparents on the farm. It succeeded.

In that school, we were also reminded that our nation was settled as a direct result of Christendom's reformation in the 16th century. Atlantic coast colonies, later coming up with state constitutions, were adamant in keeping religious heritage in its language.

The Christian ethic, in all its beliefs, reigned supreme through the 1950s. I remember arthritic women, before the era of church busses, walking a one way, sultry mile to worship in a half finished building, tithing what they could little afford.

Today, our youth is eager to follow the Christian teaching of "be perfect." At an early age they begin with the T-H-E syndrome, the cost of which is footed by mom and dad. With beauty and secularism comes the declaration of "I am perfect; I need no gods before me." Yet, they will often enter a church with friends if entertainment and a four string guitar is on the podium. Jesus is out: God is in (which includes Islam and Zen Buddhism): "Yea, God!" The church leaders (group psychologists) are happy.

With medical "new parts for old" technology, the quest for immortality continues. The media spotlights patients who have more than 3 or 4 transplanted organs.[*]

We are a nation that must have its "buzz" words or phrases for entertainment. They enter our lexicon for a year or two, then disappear in favor of something introduced by television, a young celebrity or other fickle source. In 1968, "right on" surfaced; in 1977, it wasn't a word, but a gesture of four fingers in the air representing quotation marks; in 2003, "that'll work" reigned.

Our buzz word for the present is "makeover" which is often stretched to "extreme" makeover. Referring to surgical changes to one's brief exterior or façade, which goes above and beyond the T-H-E syndrome.

Self esteem blooms for the "makeoveree," but using whose yardstick to measure confidence and values? What can be said of an angel or Greek god who cannot utter a word when an unexpected voice answers the phone?

The Greeks, et al, had a lot to say about beauty, and some of their nuances point to redefining it. But alas, you'll not find them discussed except perhaps in a small private college.

---

[*] NBC News, September 22, 2005.

THE MIND

Will humankind redefine beauty, equate it to "immortality" and seek it through surgery, drugs and robot worship? The Greeks await and deserve an answer.

7. Dogs (and Kids) Rule

As a preteen I had my first dog, an Irish Shepherd which my father thought might be fun to take along on hunting trips. Like most members of the canine family, it had the usual healthy and normal drives: curiosity, geniality and constant hunger.

When dad was engaged in an intricate household job requiring concentration, the dog often came nosing in to investigate. Knowing I was nearby, the old man would call out: "Put the dog where it belongs or I'll chain it."

The dog, who answered to "Fabian." Had a large, utilitarian kennel, but during the second year, his sex drive evidently caused him to jump the fence and disappear for a few days. Heartsick, I left his door open and, sure enough, one night I heard a telltale moan that he was back.

A quick examination with the flashlight laid me low. An auto, truck or something had broken his mandible and gangrene had set in. His entire head was swollen. My touch brought howls of pain. The next day was Sunday; that afternoon, I got busy.

Dad was away on company assignment, so I took charge of the inevitable. Selecting a gravesite in our soft garden soil, I went down about three feet until I hit clay. I joined two apple crates with poplar planking and lined the makeshift coffin with an old quilt half destined for the kennel.

Before going to bed, I called on retired friend and next-door neighbor, Emmit, who had hunted with us and knew Fabian... the dog would show no fear of him. I took my Winchester shotgun plus two rounds of "duck loads" (#4 shot) and told him the tearful story of what had to be done—tomorrow. His misty eyes said what he couldn't. He just took the weapon, nodded and gave me a hug.

With cotton-plugged ears, I tossed and turned that night. The following morning, I was at school early, but learned nothing all day. I could picture Emmit's agony with such a job, and it made me love him.

I got home late, just in time for supper. Mom, who knew every detail, put her arms around me and pointed to the cleaned shotgun with a returned duck load that Emmit hadn't needed. He had mounded the grave beautifully and installed a neat white, wooden cross that endured until we moved from there.

It was 41 years before I had another dog.

The elevation of pet status in the United States has been a long time coming. Needless to say, their position in American society today is unique worldwide.

During my last extensive trip to China in the 1980s, pet ownership was forbidden. Reason? Too much wasted time and resources. One of my translators, however, did admit to a kitten while in large cities—away from prying eyes.

Koreans, in some provinces, were different. They fattened certain dog breeds for an annual feast... which continues today.

Canines were also edible fare in Mexico. When the Pontiac broke down near Monterrey in 1953, our overnight host offered delectable looking hindquarters.

In the 1930s, Hollywood's Walt Disney began with Mickey Mouse, but was elemental, as his empire grew, in convincing us that our pets talked and communicated with us. MGM's Lassie series fueled the fire, not to mention all the self-respecting cowboy heroes with horses that took and executed orders.

Enter Benjamin Spock with his baby and childcare book in 1945. By 1970, he had been blamed for our permissive society of the sixties, but every kiddie who wanted a doggie got one—or four. The objective, said Ben, was to have family fun. Just strap them on your back, dog or baby, and climb Ayers Rock in Australia's red desert. One can always have more babies and buy or acquire more dogs.*

Pets now star in our frame-a-second color TV commercials, with computer technology to make them speak, perform gymnastics and fly. Owners build homes

---

* Ayers Rock near Alice Springs in Australia's red desert is a smooth sand blasted monolith with few hand holds rising several hundred feet above he plain. A big tourist attraction, it has a small "warning museum" near its base which displays graphic photos of the fallen, kids and adults. When I climbed it in the early 1990s, I was surprised, but not shocked, by the number of young parents eager to take tots, ages 1-3 in harms way.

or reject new ones with pets in mind. In 2003, they spent 8.6 billion dollars on them, including portraits, resorts and psychiatry. "DOGS RULE" has become the most requested auto vanity license plate.

Kid entertainment is important to mom and dad. Since 2002, Chrysler-Daimler has gone out of its way to let them travel in style. Called a "brat hauler" in private by company executives, the 4-5 passenger car has a conspicuously elevated rear seat, enabling the little ones to direct traffic and identify the next stop. Sales are soaring.

8. Media Shame

Who among the informed can deny that Corporate America is a synonym for the nation's media? No one. Its near treasonable objective is to entertain the American public while in an engineered atmosphere of "cash back bargains."

This hypnosis, coupled with the greater part of our retirees on a regimen of mind-altering drugs, gives Big Brother a Carte Blanche to rush to globalization. Many of the country's retired leaders and educators are aware of the avarice which is the driving force behind a coming decadence. They remember our heritage and feel our sovereignty slipping; still, they say nothing.

Today, a Congressional Senate Committee is deeply into a study that will "justify" a North American Union, both economically and geographically, a cut above the European Union which preserves borders and, in some countries, currency.

The proposal: Borders come down and there are no trade restrictions (because of NAFTA, FTAA and CAFTA, there are few now; the American public has been "indoctrinated".) The Pan American dollar is born, along with a central government for this hemisphere. For the first 100 years, guess who picks up the neighbor's health care tab?

Globalization, control of world affairs covertly, through the United Nations, has long been the dream of heady neo-cons that meet annually at a specified resort. To certain historians and journalists, the group known as Bildlerberg (see Chapter 9.)

Ultimately the objective is pooling and control of the earth's resources through the merging of three major spheres of influence: a) North and South America; b) Europe-Africa; c) Asia-Pacific (which would include Indonesia and Australia).

Are world inhabitants ready for the demise of nationalism? For a robot-like existence where doles and mediocre health care reign? Where "quality of life" must be redefined?

Abundant data on these proposals are available online, but why does the media keep us in the dark? A few psychologists think "the American public is not yet ready; more 'conditioning' is needed. The third-world stigma must be eliminated."

Well, while "conditioning" is administered, the media needs to debate or, at least, surface reports of nuclear weapons in the hands of terrorists within our borders.

Retired members of the U.S. Intelligence community say that Al-Qaida nukes are already among us; that both terrorists and bombs were smuggled across the Mexican border with the help of street gangs and organized crime.

The detonation plan, according to the report, is called the "American Hiroshima" and will include multiple bombs procured by Al-Qaida from the former Soviet Union in the form of suitcase nukes and nuclear mines. The "inevitable assault" is designed to kill millions, destroy the economy and fundamentally alter the course of history.*

If the report is bogus, why isn't the source challenged—or arrested?

---

* WorldNetDaily.com, July 11, 2005. Joseph Farah's G-2 Bulletin.

9. Bilderberg

Under the heading of Globalism, American taxpayers—that includes all of us—should be briefed on the Bilderberg Group. It's a shadowy cabal which takes its name from the hotel in Holland where it first met in 1954. Its objective: to control the world's bottom line, of course.

The confab meets annually at various locations around the world, always in extreme secrecy, often at resorts controlled by either the Rockefeller or Rothchild families.

Most prominent attendees are west European royalty, members of the above families, world citizen, Henry Kissinger, and board members of Corporate America's propaganda voices, the New York Times, the Wall Street Journal, et al. The mainstream media prints not a word about events or attendees. Security is legendary; you could lose your camera or front teeth.

In July 2005, a group of 8 nations (G8) met at Gleneagles, Scotland. President Bush was there; so were the Bilderbergers, pushing a global tax proposal pending before the United Nations. The tax on oil would be designed to throw more money at world poverty—through the UN. After all, the African community can't work for global industry if under nourished.

While the USA practically supports UN operating expenses, Bilderberg, at Gleneagles, argued for more: 0.7

percent of our gross national income, as opposed to .115 which we're now paying. The Bush administration displayed no resistance to this power grab. The increased tax on oil would be presented to an unsuspecting public at the pump.[3]

In the meantime, enjoy your Hummers, America.

10. Avarice*

When I was a teenager, my father worked for a large manufacturing company; the president and general manager (today's CEO) took a liking to me and I practically had a bedside prerogative with him.

As I learned about business, mostly through popular movies of the time, his trust in me prompted a question while alone in his office. I knew about the Board of Directors and his responsibility to them, so I wanted to know about the company's profit margin.

His assessment: "The Board knows that we can invest surplus capital and get a 6% return on, say municipal bonds (before WW II), but worldwide business prospects being what they are convinced me we can aim for a 15% return without losing public trust." (The term "consumer confidence" had not yet arrived.) He was genuinely proud of that mark.

Fifteen percent!!!!!!!!!!!?????????? According to modern CEOs, such a margin wouldn't even go the broom closet in a new office building, let alone, pay the CEO's salary.

---

* I first used this word for articles and reports in 1957. That same year, Hollywood, in filming Ernest Hemingway's, "The Sun Also Rises," used the word "impotent" to describe the hero Jake Barnes' medical problem after WW I. It sent American scurrying for the dictionary; this may be a reprise.

Avarice is a state of mind and to the boomers who were raised on a steady diet of "somebody owes me this," an American manufacturing revolution was duck soup.

Here's an example: The product is a collared, golf shirt with two pockets, one monogrammed. The following year, with the dollar and market stable, the monogram is omitted, same price. The following year, it becomes a one pocket shirt, same price. The following year, pocket is omitted, same price. The following year, the collar disappears (it becomes a T-shirt), same price.

This formula, coupled with ever rising "great society" personnel expense, brought about "down-sizing" (dumb-sizing) in the 1980s. Corporate profits were still inadequate, so Congress passed the NAFTA which authorized the destruction of middle class America by exporting jobs to both Canada and Mexico. A year later, the FTAA legislation brought every site from Punta Arenas, Chile to Bogotá, Columbia into the fold. This year, Central America, via the CAFTA (it passed the House by two votes) completed the hemispheric circuit.

11. Image

Recently, I gave a neighbor's son a lift to the big city, armed with a new driver's license, the high school grad was "chewing at the bit" to own his first car. He had to be vocal about it and I let him talk; it was news I could use.

We were soon bogged down in interstate traffic and I chided his eagerness by asking a Frank Sinatraism: "For one-million dollars, how many new cars are added to the American interstate system each year? No response (I had expected: "Don't know; don't care!"), so I laid it on him. "Over 30 million, but you'll not see or hear that on ABC, CBS or NBC."

"What's that got to do with me?" he countered. "That's what I want." Pointing to a Hummer II in the next lane. "It's my IMAGE!"

"But you don't have a job, and that's a $3.00 per gallon gas guzzler."

"It doesn't matter. My grandparents will get it for me."

Weeks later, they did.

This story is not unique. My neighbor is a boomer and this kid his product, taught to expect MORE because he's "special." If we click and go back one window, we'll find his parents are preparing for the same—a four-car garage, five-bedroom home totaling 12,000 square feet of living space.

A statement-maker made possible by state-of-the-art technology, it will be highly visible on high ground and composed mostly of pressure-treated pine, "yellow wood," vinyl, glass, synthetic marble, various fiberglass and formaldehyde wraps and low density, colored brick veneer. Developers do not tell insurance providers that it will not prevail against a 60 knot wind; however, it is their IMAGE.

Too, their classmates have ways of broadcasting where they are coming from: a) A contemporary "Twelve Oaks" fronted by 20 acres of cotton which is never harvested; b) Front lawn pastures sport thoroughbreds which are never ridden or sold; and c) Costly airplanes in special hangars which are not flown.

I well remember a young boomer couple's dilemma: How to get an ancient armor cabinet from the MD dealer to their New York City home. A pickup truck was available, but the vehicle violated principles of IMAGE and a station wagon was rented.

A few years later, auto industry psychologist assuaged the generation's requirement by coming up with a high riding muscle car with limited hauling capability; the on-demand SUV was born.

We all have something to say in the way we dress and appear in public—message T-shirts excepted. In the 1960s, youth wanted to transfer Woodstock to fashion, and it did temporarily until our garment districts (before China, et al) saw adults rebel at the slovenliness mixed with business.

IMAGE today is subtler. Or is it? Women want blonde locks, false nails (hand and foot), tight jeans and zircons on their flip-flops—AFTER the T-H-E syndrome is absolved. Men, especially sports figures, compete with face hairstyles. They are not the Rutherford B. Hayes, George Armstrong Custer or U.S. Grant configurations; rather, care is taken to ignore the Burt Reynolds mustache of yesterday and come up with the most bizarre Fu Man Chu imaginable. Beauty is in the beholder and women, thus far, have not objected to male decorations.

Tattoos are an image label; they usually say what the wearer is unable to convey through speech or action. In the 1930s, Tattooing proliferated in the Orient and sailors in our growing Navy brought them home.

Not everybody approved. Religious institutions generally taught that to decorate and alter the body was to violate Natural Law, a trust given by a Higher Power; therefore, to wear tattoos was to mock the commandments of home, family, and religion—easy for a criminal mind.

Enter the 1970s: Parental hatred and secularism threw such rules out the window…. Add to that, the march of technology which made the art safe, painless and more colorful.

Recently, I stood in a post office line behind a tall man in his 20s. His neck had been shaved so the new tattoo, his lifelong bumper sticker to the world, stood out like a neon sign. In the shape of a Christian cross, it invited me to fornicate with myself.

12. Fear

Let's set the stage for a less populous, safer summertime: The windows were open, fans going; retired residents or housewives sat on the front porch and talked with the immediate neighbor, 30 feet away; noise pollution was non-existent. The iceman came and went.

Citizens kept informed by the AM radio and 3-cent newspapers (editorial opinions conflicted). The recent buzz word was "kidnapping," spawned by the Lindbergh tragedy and subsequent execution of the guilty.

Still, in most American cities, there was no paranoia. People were confident, sincere and secure—a galvanization that would see them through to ultimate victory in the coming war.

For those who could afford them, telephones were a convenience and curiosity. The instrument usually occupied a central niche where sitting down was not an option, since conversations were deliberately kept short to appease others on the party line.

Municipal street lighting was not universal. If you got off the streetcar and walked home after dark, a pocket flashlight could prevent a sprained ankle. If someone loomed up out of the darkness, a greeting of "Hi" or "Excuse me" usually followed. During such an era, women, walking alone, felt safe.

And we were amiable. People struck up conversations on trolleys, busses and trains to exchange information or to pass the time. Elders were honored and the excess energy of kids attenuated (The anti-thesis of Benjamin Spock).

Enter the godless, encapsulated society of today: People, endowed the luxuries of television and air-conditioning, went indoors and kept track of their neighbors by reading obituaries. Orwellian instruction proceeded, the ACLU appeared and Americans were told how to evaluate a person, place or thing—in 10-color process.

Today, the most common emotion which pervades and permeates American society is FEAR. True, it is rampant, in part, as a result of the "nine-eleven" terrorist attacks, but the cause runs far deeper.

Most Americans are aware of that part of the Constitution known as the Bill of Rights. Even if not well read, they also know that these basic rights have been diluted, replaced, usurped (choose your verb) by legislation and by that flawed ideology contrived by the nation's campuses: The scourge of political correctness. Still, they say nothing.

Following the Civil Rights Act of 1964, civil service and state municipal jobs became a target for discrimination claims—up 2,200 percent between 1969 and 1994. When efficiency suffered, a paranoid silence settled over the workplace. Only a fool said what he actually believed. It was too easy to be misunderstood or have your words taken out of context.

As the population burgeoned and the sea of human rights deepened, other classes, through new and "just" interpretation of the law, sought protection through legislation: White men over 40, short people, the chemically addicted, the left-handed, the obese, members of all religions, et al.

In 1975, Congress passed what was to become The Individuals with Disabilities Education Act. The act gave disabled children right to "specially designed instruction," at no cost to parents or guardians, to meet the unique needs of a handicapped child. State budgets crumbled.

Wheelchair users who wished to enter the mainstream now made their move through lobbies. Forty-three million strong in 1990, they got the Americans with Disabilities Act which let them:

a) Hold up a rush hour Manhattan bus for fifteen minutes while ONE rider got on board. Demand all busses be modified.

b) Sit by an airliner's emergency exit window.

c) Demand that all hockey rinks make the scorer's box wheelchair accessible; that all sport stadiums be ramp modified.

d) Sue ALL establishments, public or private, for discrimination.

Budgets didn't just crumble—they self-destructed. Citizens sensed a definite spurt in their taxes; still, they said nothing.[4]

In Federalist Paper 51, James Madison spoke of the problems of men governing men, of just control of the governed, of government controlling itself.

This last is most important. But rights are not the language of democracy, and the government that hands them out on demand abdicates its prerogatives and loses its ability to control the governed.

So, this is a thumbnail view of how we have, in 40 stressful years, become a nation of enemies—mostly palm upward. It can get worse; hence, the person on the street in Punxsutawney, PA or Chadron, NB, the strap hanger in New York or Chicago, keeps the eyes wide and the ears back, hoping their words will not be deciphered through binoculars or that they will not be ear-marked by thought police.

Shades of fear in Nazi Germany, 1933.

13. Guilt

In the corridors of the human brain, the labyrinth of the guilt complex ranges far and wide. In the world of psychoanalysis, guilt in a patient is common, but responses to stimuli are hard to predict.

Unscrupulous stimuli are alive and well on Sunday morning television, appealing to the basic American ethics of yesteryear: Family, work and religion, especially the latter. The group of arthritic ladies who walked to church and tithed beyond their means (see chapter 6.) ... they and their like are gone today; still, this is the never-ending age group targeted by palm upward institutions... which are never-ending.

Although its message has varied, one organization has used a single post office box for forty years plus. Competing with requests for relief from a brace of devastating hurricanes this year, it will undoubtedly return in their wake with renewed vigor.

In the pre-Spock era, parental teachings, ages one through four laid a groundwork which said that faith alone would suffice to gain the kingdom of God; however, if one could not support the church with regular attendance, GOOD WORKS would absolve this requirement.

Thus, was Protestant America, often backed up by quoted scripture, never forgotten by a benevolent brotherhood of Sunday morning media solicitors.

The good life and great society cometh. The citizen's time was demanded by secular discoveries. Christians and other devotees had to make room for video games, computers, cruises and endless forms of instant, complete gratification.

Never mind that thy neighbor's job had been shipped south and abroad by our well meaning leaders through programs like the NAFTA, the FTAA and the CAFTA.[*] Not to worry; just make your contribution and sleep well.

---

[*] If not up to speed on the acronyms, consult the glossary.

14. Race

"You can not legislate love."

I attribute that statement to the friend and boss of the African American I'm about to praise. The nation's lawmakers and "Leaders" insist that interracial love and respect was not possible until the government interceded—the Civil Rights Act of 1964. Not true.

In 1934, kidnapping was an ugly word. The Lindbergh tragedy was unwinding; a suspect was in prison and a trial ongoing. In our home there was no paranoia; at age three, following a thorough briefing from my father, I was given the full range of an unfenced yard.

City utility departments during that era operated without powerful backhoes and hydraulic "cherry picker" cranes; it was mostly pick and shovel technology. When two giant black men came to the edge of our lot to install a new water-metering valve, it got my attention.

Their mission, as I deduced in later years, was to dig a hole deep enough and large enough to permit the bricklayers to line the site for a new metered valve. It was a hot day, and I must have amused them, a chattering kid in "rompers"… blonde from head to toe… but one who didn't get in the way.

The larger guy was the pick man. With every stroke, he emitted a loud "huuggh"—a strong exhalation that seemed to push out every cubic centimeter of lung air.

The soil gave way to his great strength. After a dozen strokes, he stepped aside for the shovel man who began to build his pile. I supervised every cycle and, in my mind's eye, labeled them "Mutt and Jeff."

Lunch time came, Mutt and Jeff, in the shade of a maple, opened their brown bags and sat down. I went inside and Mom, aware of my newly found interest, gave me two wedges from a raisin pie she had just baked. Upon delivery, our friendship flourished.

That afternoon, Jeff told me about his boy my age and their dog. Mutt, the talkative, storyteller of the two, wove a tale that had me wide-eyed. It seems that the best source of puppy dogs was right over our heads. Every block wired for electricity had a gray metal box that measured about two feet high and a foot in diameter (a power transformer), and in each box was a genuine, loving puppy just waiting to be taken.

Before going to bed that night, I divulged the secret to dad. He smiled, tucked me in and said nothing.

I was sad when, after two days, Mutt and Jeff finished and moved to operating air hammers half a block away. But at lunchtime, they would come sit under the maple tree, offer me tidbits from the paper sacks, and tease me about not having a dog.

The summer moved on; by now they were working the macadam road in the next block. Then there was a period of days in which I failed to show; it must have been family imposed quarantine due to chicken pox or perhaps the time when I recuperated from a nasty fall down the cellar steps.

Nonetheless, I remember that late afternoon knock on the door which my mother answered. From my room I heard the voices of Mutt and Jeff, Mom's laughter and the sound of nails clawing and slipping on a hardwood floor. They disappeared and she appeared before me with a hungry and scrambling puppy in her arms. Their message: "We robbed one of the boxes… get well soon."

The "Heinz 57" pup was clean and healthy, but didn't last long. Dad argued he had no time to build an appropriate kennel… that he would get me the right dog at the right time. Still, I'll never forget my first, however temporary, puppy dog.

During WW II, my father served in the Army's Corps of Engineers. We moved often and I knew many blacks and Hispanics. But it was not until after age 20, when I entered the Air Force, that indelible relationships ensued.

Otis Air Force Base, Massachusetts, 1952: I became crew chief for a Lockheed F-94 Starfighter Interceptor. It wasn't supersonic, but with rockets and an afterburner, it was a formidable opponent should Soviet bombers come calling across Canada. The cold war was real.

As crew chief, I was responsible for one aircraft's airworthiness… to meet with the pilot before and after a sortie; to advise him on previous maintenance and aircraft history, and to get his signature when appropriate; to ground test a new engine when installed; to see that the aircraft was serviced with the proper quality and quantity of fuel as required. While awaiting appointment as an aviation cadet and flying training, I thought this to be the Air Force's best job.

Before the age of missiles, interceptors were important after Russia got the bomb. Otis was important because of its proximity to "the range," a section of shallow sea off Cape Cod where targets of "variety" could be used and the results photographed. During summer months, F-94/F-89 crews of two, pilot and radar observer, were ordered to temporary duty at Otis.

Standing out among them was a tall, 6'4", black captain who came from Tyndall Air Force Base, Florida. Picture a "Joe Louis," only more handsome. With the front cockpit seat adjusted to the "full down" position, he barely fit the airplane. Once he flew my F-94, he always returned to it. I think he liked its maintenance history.

His uniform cap size must have been seven and five eights to three quarters. While his observer was a full inch smaller. My routine preflight duties, once they were in the cockpits, included handing them their individual crash helmets complete with oxygen masks. To get a rise out of him, I frequently mixed them up. Nothing… until about the fifth faux pas, he said, "Sergeant, each has a name on it; get on the stick."

His last sortie with me was near Thanksgiving, and he seemed to sense the Air Force would promote him out of an operational pilot status. Suddenly, he admitted I had a name: "Delaney, you and your crew do good work. Thanks."

For 13 years, I didn't see him close-up, but the Air Force Times told me he was still in the Air Defense Command as a full colonel. During that period, I had gone through flying training and pulled a tenure with the Strategic Air Command.

In early 1968, the nation struggled with itself and the worst happened when Martin Luther King, Jr. was assassinated. My black friend, being a key director of the Air Force Association, was put on the spot by having to keynote the AFA's annual convention in Atlanta. Jimmy Carter, then a Georgia Senator, was our host.

The colonel, a proud member of his race, could set the stage for what was to follow so soon after the divisive King crime. But what would he say? What tone would he offer?

What he said, when introduced by Jimmy Carter, was a landmark speech for the time. He acknowledged the terror which gripped his heart as well as ours; he challenged us not to over-react to the crime of a small minority. Then he searched his own soul by promising to "stand up for her (his nation) through thick and thin."

Later, in that Atlanta hotel, I cornered him long enough to offer congratulations. We were both in uniform with nametags. I then said: "Colonel, you don't remember me, but I... " Quickly, he shut me off with a raise of the hand. Then, towering over me with the hint of a smile, he declared: "The hell I don't, Delaney. You're the Otis buy who always gave me the wrong sized brain bucket!"

He inquired about my career, training and plans, taking a break from his busy schedule. In parting, he crushed my hand in his and I felt genuine camaraderie.

Later, we both had exposure to the Vietnam War, his being far more distinguished than mine. As the war came to an end I found myself in the Pentagon as a manager of Airlift Resources. The morale of the next-of-kin to POWs and MIAs weighed heavily on President Nixon, and he brought them to Washington once annually through 1973.

Bob Dole, then congressman from Kansas, became Nixon's choice to brief the NOKs from all 50 states once they got to the nation's capital. Getting them there via Air Force airlift became the responsibility of my black colonel friend, now a Brigadier General. I learned later, he personally selected me to arrange the nuts and bolts of the 12-squadron mission, setting up routes and tasking the necessary units.

It was an exacting job for all concerned, using taxpayer dollars while trying to meet varying needs of individual requests from the NOK. Because of its acoustics, Constitution Hall became the site for Dole briefings. One evening, with a morning departure scheduled for most attendees, I stood in an antechamber taking notes when the General appeared at my elbow. His aide stood 50 feet away.

"How's it going, Delaney?" I gave him a quick briefing on who was and wasn't there, and the status of all transports scheduled for a next day departure. He took off his wet raincoat.

I didn't have to get near to know he had been drinking heavily; I could smell the whiskey. At this point of his career, he was the Air Force's pinup boy, and the social and public affairs expectations had to be met, or so he thought.

We were alone so, surprising myself, I laid it on the line: "General, with all due respect, Sir, you shouldn't go in there. You've had a lot to drink, and you'll be talking one on one with some of the NOKs; if I can smell it, so can they. Why don't you have your aide drive you home?"

He looked me up and down then thought for a moment. He said not a word; just handed me the raincoat and I helped him into it. I saw him leave in his staff car.

Fast forward to 1977 at the Air University, Montgomery, Alabama. After a 10-month residency at the Air War College as a Lieutenant Colonel, I was to graduate in a couple of weeks. As a class from all services and five countries, we had been lectured and inspired by the likes of Henry Kissinger, Curtis LeMay and then CIA chief, George H. Bush.

Now, as Commander, Air Defense Command, with headquarters at Cheyenne Mountain, Ent Air Force Base, Colorado, my friend was coming to do the same, but from the view of a black four star general.

He made history by being the Air Force's first, mastering every job given him, including foreign liaison, while asking for more, he added three stars in four years. The college commander knew of our trails crossing over the years and asked me to be his "bat man" while on station—a job I relished.

We had little time privately and it was no surprise. He was on the phone constantly when not lecturing and answering student questions. Too, the physical strain and drain of the last four years was evident; he had gained 20 pounds and the boom in his voice had faded.

As new AF missiles replaced our air defense system, my friend retired from active duty. But civilian life was unkind to him and his health deteriorated; he died prematurely of a cardiac problem.

Today, as African-Americans debate or pontificate on issues, I often ask myself: "What would my general have to say about it? Yes, a month seldom goes by where I don't reminisce and recount those special days with my friend and hero, Daniel "Chappie" James.

15. School Days

The year 1938 knew many momentous events: Congress authorized funds for a two-ocean Navy; Britain's Prime Minister Chamberlain signed that infamous and worthless document with Adolph Hitler which guaranteed "peace in our time;" Pilot Douglas Corrigan took off from New York bound for the west coast and landed in Ireland. He blamed the dilemma on "compass error." But his personality and subsequent book made him a celebrity and all was forgiven.

But for me, the most momentous 1938 event was my entry into a truly rural, public school at age seven. Although beyond my formative years, it would provide lifelong lessons and values.

The nation, three years the other side of Pearl Harbor, still struggled with the great depression. Although President Roosevelt and a balanced congress had known moderate success in putting the "forgotten man" back to work, times were hard and our capital city was no exception.

Consumerism, as we know it today was non-existent; everything was made in the USA. When product demand*

---

* Actually, demand for new products remained, but a credit card world, it wasn't. During the great depression, you made do with what you had. I remember 25 year old Ford "Tin Lizzies" being resurrected... trucks from the WW I era, with solid rubber tires and chain drive, back on the road.

vanished, manufacturing plants cut back and my father was a victim.

The family gave up its two-story, four-bedroom, big city house and elected to move in temporarily with my paternal grandparents, 80 miles east... My father knew the hardware business well and there, in this small town, he found work.

Before WW II, the railroad was king, and because it passed through the town, it bustled. Blessed by both a US highway and two daily railroad stops, the town became a magnet for the locals. The single general merchandise storekeeper had a two-story building full of locally butchered meat, plow points, mule "bonnets" (bridles) and galvanized washtubs. Because money was scarce, he advanced credit on huge folding ledgers to all he knew. One problem: The quality public school was 10 miles distant and bussing was not yet on the budget-annihilating drawing board. (Every educational dollar allocated the state went toward teacher salaries, text books and buildings—as opposed to politics.)

My only sibling, an older sister who labeled me her "little brother," and I would have a problem getting to "Plain View," reputed to be a "progressive school" worth attending. Fortunately, the school's principal and his member of the faculty wife were practically next door neighbors and sister Betty and I fitted nicely into the back seat of their new black Ford V-8.

As a third grader, I was impressed with Plain View, primarily because of its rural setting and its discipline which kept in step with my father's regimen. In that department, I would excel where others had problems.

My teacher was a lady of Irish lineage who taught three grades concurrently in her south room. She had a big heart, but ruled like an unsmiling drill sergeant. A potbellied cast iron stove provided winter heat. The school's well and its outdoor plumbing were widely separated.

One dark, rainy morning, a fellow classmate came in late; he appeared exhausted from milking chores. Our teacher was more than distressed. Not only did she scold him publicly for showing up late with dirty hands, she made him heat water in a one pound coffee can atop the stove and wash before the class. Tears streamed from his swollen, sleepless eyes, but no one made a sound.

When recess came, we opened our lunch pails or sacks and, weather permitting, went outside. Who needed park type swings, seesaws or gym bars? We had our imaginations! One boy would stiffen his right arm, rotate it like a propeller and disappear on a half hour flight through knee high sage grass. During the Fall, some of us would gather still green walnuts, crush them between stones and have dessert. (The stain on our hands remained for weeks and I heard from my father about it.)

The school building's two wings were separated by an assembly area and a small stage, probably developed later as a gymnasium. During the school year, the county board held two evening assemblies, Fall and Spring, where "box suppers" were auctioned off. Proceeds went into a fund that insured continuance.

THE MIND

My grandfather, a Spanish-American War veteran and Baptist minister, whose voice could be heard and heeded a quarter mile away, served as auctioneer. He announced the name of each lady preparing the supper and bidding proceeded accordingly. It was a social opportunity and many single adults attended.

With a typical third grade appetite, I remember well the box contents: Fried chicken, ham or pork chops; baking powder biscuits or corn bread; boiled eggs, sweet or sour pickles; two cake slices or pie wedges per box; plenty of butter and fruit preserves on a side table.

The frequent suppers became a prime event for dancing, but none occurred. There appeared to be an aura of gratification, and I often heard men talking a little business. Still, the depression weighed heavily upon us.

Generations later, while looking at the annual class picture, (8 x 10 black and white shot on the school lawn), one can see it in our eyes… questioning and unsure.

Today, third and fourth graders do not have that look of anxiety. Indeed, it has been replaced with a gleam in the eyes that the leader of Nazi youth would have cherished. They do not revere male pilots that flew solo across oceans, nor do they want to hear or read about them. The European-American male, despite history books, was evil itself, and is to be ridiculed and lampooned in all meaningful television commercials and sitcoms.

Too, the Constitution's first amendment goes too far in free speech. The Boy Scouts of America is a chip off the old block and must be reformed… the Sierra Club is a much better choice for youth and the outdoors. Heroes are to be replaced with heroines such as Betty Friedan, Marilyn Manson and Doris K. Goodwin. Diversity does not lead to mediocrity; it is the backbone of political correctness.

Recently, a six year old, tired of his teacher talking back, hit her with a well-aimed, unopened, can of cola. It drew blood and onlookers cheered. The story, carried the following day by a moderate newspaper, drew hundreds of letters and phone calls from educated, thinking parents, all with a main thrust question: "Why didn't the principal call Mom or Dad and demand: 'Come get your kid!'" It turns out the principal did consider the obvious; however, being a Benjamin Spock advocate, he pronounced the kid a temporary neurotic and shrugged the event off.

Today, my third grade teacher would laughingly be dismissed as the "Irish Mafia." Her psyche could never be matriculated into godless, permissive public schools. Protestant church unions once exhibited great influence in education; however, secular changes and subtle nuances, telegraphed by Corporate America via the television medium, have made them impotent—from total Bible sales to public display of the Ten Commandments.

Aside from interviews, I seldom solicit inputs from fellow retired educators; however, two late ones warrant inclusion here.

The nation's overwhelming preoccupation with diversity through flawed ideologies can lead to expensive consequences, leader embarrassment and mediocrity. Under the heading of education, I cite two of the many states now submerged in the standard Orwellian dictum.

A retired New York City educator reflects on his 25 years of freedom to show personal slides of the Holy Land during periods prior to Easter/Passover/Christmas/Hanukkah, etc. Parents did not object. Every year, his students included Jews, Catholics, Protestants, Muslims and Hindus.

In the Big Apple today, teacher freedom has been replaced by "the Gestapo" breathing down teacher's neck. The mayor's education chancellor is not an educator, but a trained intimidator. He or she commands a staff of inspectors who make the rounds often to write up teachers and principals for such check points as seating arrangements and bulletin boards; even veteran, old guard teachers are harassed.[5]

North Carolina, since it became a state, has been known for excellence in two endeavors: furniture manufacture and education. In both genres, it has fallen from grace. The former, due to a worldwide lack of quality wood; the latter, dictated by Corporate America under the guise of political correctness.

The nonprofit, nonpartisan Pope Center for Higher Education, based in Raleigh, uncovered the following about the state's 11 largest institutions:

a) Not one requires undergraduates to take a course in U.S. history.

b) Only one-third require a course in Western Civilization or Western history.

c) Almost two-thirds require a course in multiculturalism or Cultural Diversity—often code words for classes that deny America's virtues and magnify its weaknesses.

d) Fewer than half require an introductory course in literature

e) Only one-third require English majors to take a course on Shakespeare, widely considered the greatest figure in English literature.

This is not to indict North Carolina. Truly, all across the land, in all subjects, the bar has been lowered.[6]

16. D-I-V-O-R-C-E

"The full measure of love is what one is willing to give up for it."

Aristotle

There has been only one memorable in my family, but it warrants repeating and analysis.

In the early 20th century, photographic portraiture was at its zenith. The glass plate negative, hand polished lenses and custom made bellows cameras insured treasured results. These portraits were the specialty of my maternal grandfather who has a studio in a capital city of 110,000.

In 1912, my grandmother who has been the "belle" of her hometown 60 miles to the east, gave birth to their fifth child, a son. As she became heftier and more pensive, she listened to idle gossip and suspicion crept into her daily mindset. On the surface, it appeared justified.

Women, both married and single, sought grandfather's studio expertise and kept coming back for more… of what I don't know.[*] Nevertheless, my grandmother

---

[*] In the 1950s, I spent considerable time with my grandfather in Los Angeles county once he retired as a still photographer with MGM studios. Alert and ambulatory until his death at age 90, he assured me his private studio back east had not been a love nest- that events which led to his flight west (and divorce) were brought on by my grandmother's imagination.

worked herself up to an undying enmity, and made the mistake of not keeping her suspicions within the family, i.e., disclosing her dilemma to brothers and sisters only.

Instead, her Welsh temper made her vocal and she broadcast to neighbors one and all that justice would be done if she had to mete it out herself with an ax while he slept. Apparently, one attempt was made, for he appeared one morning before the county constable suffering from a nasty shoulder wound with a story that no one of that era wanted to hear.

No complaints were filed, yet he met with the editor of the county newspaper the following day before boarding a train for Nevada. The year was 1916.

Then, as now, Nevada was a divorce fountainhead, the person filing needing only six weeks residency. Conduct that constitutes grounds for divorce varies from state to state, and Nevada was quite liberal in defining criminal intent. My grandfather, through affidavits from constable, editor, et al, was rendered a favorable judgment.

Divorce rate in America (divorces per 1,000 population) has generally risen since the 1920s; it peaked at 5.3 in 1981 before declining somewhat. As we entered the new millennium, the rate stood at 4.2. The decline is a product of several inputs which can easily be explored by the reader.

The marriage contract today, as we become more secular, can be a written agreement almost completely devoid of religious tradition, and drawn up by attorneys of the principals. Bride and groom often write their own "marriage vows." The contract goes so far at the time of union to identify "who gets what" should a break come. Little is said about a "legal separation" or "separate maintenance"… it is a boom or bust approach. Hence, when a divorce occurs, hyphenated names remain, and the split may not appear on the rolls.

Drugs, the darling of Corporate America, also contribute to a decline in divorce. In the 1990s, divorce in the age group 55-65 soared. Case histories revealed that the problem may have been more than simply testosterone versus estrogen. Wives were losing control; men felt they had been reduced to consort duty… implying: "There's more to life than shopping and waiting in the wings during gossip sessions." To preserve the union, husbands got more than sensitivity lectures. They got organic chemistry's solution to humankind's problems—the proper drug.*

The cellular phone has also helped to preserve unions. Recently, I traveled across state by car with a male friend, married for 35 years. It was a three-hour drive and, since he liked driving, I retreated to the vacant back seat, sorted a stack of papers and wrote.

---

* In 2000, a doctor friend confirmed my suspicions. I was a victim of acute depression and in a state of moderate collapse; my secondary symptom and malady was a shutdown of the adrenal system with pain so great I became a candidate for suicide. I was truly a subhuman form. Our conversation: PCP: "I can fix it so you will never appear before me again in this state." Answer: "You want to prescribe mind-altering drugs." PCP: "We don't call them that." Answer: "That's part of my problem, doc!"

He was part of a family that worshipped this relatively new system and put a great deal of money into it. Therefore, I wasn't surprised when he, 70 miles down the interstate, "reported in."

"Hello, darling. We're just passing mile 130 and should be there in a couple of hours. Jim is in the back seat working and driving weather is good. I love you. Talk to you later."

Well, "later" became the following hour, almost to the minute. I could imagine the smile on his wife's face; she had extended her tether of control—electronically.

We remained overnight in the same room (although suites were being hawked) and "reports" were made just before lights out and before a morning shower. He caught me staring at him in disbelief and blurted out: "She feels more secure when I check in periodically."

Sexual relationships supportive of a more perfect union were reported by Masters and Johnson in 1970 and again in 1982.[7] A couple of chapters should have been entitled "Sex after 60," for their guidance helped to wash away taboos ingrained during formative years that maintained that sex was for reproduction only.

Both M.D.s and psychologists, they had much to say about achieving the golden anniversary, but it remained for other psychologists to declare that 50 years of wedded bliss can be attained only when the husband, during the "problem years," remains completely subservient.

17. Religion and Politics

In the early 20th century, a popular axiom observed by all when at American social gatherings stood out: Refrain from discussing religion and politics. Otherwise, your first amendment rights could lead to a bloody nose or even grudge killings.

Devout beliefs, coupled with limited education and exposure to society, can be dangerous. You can't tell a neighbor; "If you don't believe as I do, you're going straight to hell," without expecting retribution in some form. Bathed in Christianity at the time, Hollywood furthered its cause in the 1940s with films which support this thesis. *

Today, should you meet someone who still lives by that axiom, the person should be avoided... for they are not informed. Now is the time to discuss our four freedoms—religion being paramount—and where, under multiculturalism (cultural communism), they are going.

Last year, I was part of such a discussion following a fraternal luncheon. One member was concerned that Christianity would degenerate to a point where Easter week would be represented only by a "bunny economy" and Christmas by Santa. Another claimed that Islam can't be trusted; that the militant thrust of the religion could

---

* If you are one of the few who missed Gary Cooper as SERGEANT YORK (Warner Brothers, 1943), get a VHS or DVD copy and enjoy. I envy you the experience.

some day dominate our nation. On we went. No threats were made; no blood shed.

Today, families need to be armed with information about the religious ethic that will let them discuss what's happening comfortably with any minister or cleric, including the Pope himself.*

Indeed, the Protestant churches of today are experiencing a Reformation. Look at the modern ones: They are huge, vulnerable structures build using the same technology some single families employ for 12,000 square foot private dwellings.

Surrounded by acres of thin asphalt, they stand as citadels or havens for those who come for subsidy and instruction. "Most of our people (he didn't see them as a congregation) can't pay their utility bills, but they are put to work in our vast system and subsequently survive," says one male interviewee.

The church is built around young America's need for entertainment and political correctness. Heritage and sovereignty are never addressed. Jesus is out; God (Yea God!!!) is in... which includes all faiths from Islam to Zen Buddhism to Taoism.

---

* For a well-documented treatise on the de-Christianizing America, see P. J. Buchanan's bestseller, DEATH OF THE WEST (St. Martin's, 2002). Also, Robert Spencer, ISLAM UNVEILED: Disturbing questions about the world's fastest growing faith (Encounter); ONWARD MUSLIM SOLDIERS: How Jihad still threatens America and the West (Regnery); THE POLITICALLY INCORRECT GUIDE TO ISLAM AND THE CRUSADES (forthcoming from Regnery).

The minister or leader does not attend a school of divinity, but rather one of mass psychology. Some of it is right out of Nuremberg and Leni Rifenstahl.

This group of churches will prosper because of legislation and the blessing of Corporate America. Tax incentives for the institution as well as contributors and sustainers are more than liberal.

In 2004, a group of southern Protestants, the Southern Baptist Convention (SBC) took a dip in the political pool, attacking the nation's Godless public schools, and damned near drowned. Holding its annual, conference in Indianapolis, the SBC offered a much heralded platform of: "Teach your kids at home, or in private parochial schools… public school curricula are not acceptable."

The conference began with a strong thrust in this direction. Nationally syndicated columnists such as Cal Thomas and Phyllis Scalafly elatedly provided their fine-tuned coverage and support. But by day three, it was clear to the nation that the number one witch to be cast out was not American public education, but a watered down denunciation of homosexuality. Someone/repeat/someone had met with the SBC board of directors and read them the facts of life by subsidy. Guess who?

The dutiful attack on our Godless public schools was not resurfaced during the conference of 2005.

II. THE BODY

18. Finger Food

A fine dining relic of a bygone era adorns my desk: a Sears-Roebuck table knife from my grandmother's kitchen and dining room, 1900-1905. Although used as a paperweight and paper cutter, it has utility, especially in the kitchen.

Of standard nine-inch table length, it was manufactured when the nation was at its steel zenith and quality control prevailed. The knife's rounded tip blade bears a two-piece wooden handle, stained mahogany and attached by three rivets. It isn't pretty; the blade is of weathered steel; yet, it has no nicks on wood or steel.

Brought to life with a few strokes on the straightening steel, it can easily disjoint a chicken or remove a finger. Its larger brother, the infamous 14 to 18 inch American butcher knife, responsible for so-o-o-o many domestic murders of the period, is found in Sears catalogs of the day. (Removal of this weapon from the Sears inventory failed to make murders per 100,000 residents, decline.)

Depending on the American scene and its ethnic influence, home butchering was common until the mid twentieth century when post war booms and secularism took over. These tools were necessary—part of life.

Using them in the home required a discipline Americans today deplore—responsibility. Enter the family ethic via my father: To expedite the evening meal, he would take my filled plate and cut all food into bite-sized pieces. When my growth and coordination became evident to him, he gave me careful instruction in how to use the Sears-type instruments, demonstrating their sharpness (tines of the fork were needle like) and efficiency.

I can hear my mother dreading this event. "Clarence , are you sure you aren't rushing things?" His reassurance: "It will give confidence; next year, I'll give him kitchen duties and let him clean game." And so it went. My father monitored me closely and I never bled from knife or sharp instrument misuse.

Complete table etiquette; however, later came from my uncle, not my father. Remembering the teachings of his grandmother, a single generation out of the old country, he taught me how to guard against "wasted motion" (He studied this in furniture manufacturing) by transferring a fork holding cut food to the right hand for ingestion. The knife was a pusher. A fork was never to be used for cutting except with dessert pastry.

Thanks to my uncle, I could attend a state dinner and thoroughly enjoy an artichoke before reaching its heart, or easily dissect and bone a whole broiled fish when set before me.

Today's fascination with finger food among adults was a long time coming. In the '70s, boomers with the "hate thy parents" syndrome experimented in all genres from food to sex to music. Young adults from prominent families could often be found in communes decorated with breadcrumbs, empty mayonnaise jars and sandwich meat wrappers. Came the dawn, some wanted to return home for a brief visit.

Such was the case when a retired member of the Tiffany family on Long Island fed and hosted his grandchildren and their unwashed companions. So distressed by the inability of young adults to use simple table hardware, he came up with a concise pocket-sized etiquette guide that is still in use today—by only too few.

Indeed, the noisy, expensive restaurants of today are supported by well-heeled young in their shorts, flip-flops and ball caps wolfing down baby back ribs while sauce drips from the elbows.

19. Metabolism

"White bread is the Devil and granulated sugar the neighbor of the beast."

Anonymous

When I got into human physiology and biochemistry, I gave them both up and never looked back. Unlike giving up cigarettes, the transition was quite easy.

White bread from refined flour is part of our heritage. From our seventeenth century settlers on, dark bread (it contained all the germ nutrients) represented the old country which was, to them, passé. The attitude, passed on for generations, prevailed into the 20th century and would be unchallenged today but for medical and research science refusing to knuckle under to Corporate America.

Today, the great American millers have but one message for consumers: "Hi! I'm O.K., you're O.K.; we're number one! Here is our pie recipe for the day (which contains a large measure of both offenders)."

Our youth is catching on, especially some of the M.D.s… despite fast food's rule some are speaking out, saying that even though one may have a gene that invites ileitis, the disease can be held at bay through diet. Other physicians are aware of dietetic dangers the public at large faces; still, like so may other citizens profiting from the status quo, they say nothing.

It remained, therefore, for European scientists and physicians to scold a thinking world for unflinchingly accepting the untried preservatives and additives used by food processors. Dr. Geoffrey T. Whitehouse, et al, were the whistle blowers of the 1960s.[8]

White (granulated) sugar, white flour and Plaster of Paris are similar products. Houseflies may lay eggs on all three, but no eggs will hatch. In freshman biology, we had to cultivate the common fruit fly, Drosophila melanogaster, from egg to adult, to tally physical characteristics and report on "phenotypic ratios." Raw, life sustaining, sugar was part of the larval substrate mixture.

Consider a cross section of part of the gastrointestinal tract, the small intestine, which is an area of absorption. To INCREASE the area of absorption, evolution has provided the higher mammals with peaks and valleys covered with layers of delicate cells. The GI tract is an unthinking assembly line. If a material has no utility it can't, as an unfood, be utilized, it usually comes to rest in the valley, there to serve as a future obstacle.

The Bible tells us that "through strength" we may reach an age of "four score" years. A synonym of that strength is "metabolism." Under that heading, all Homo Sapiens are not created equal. The body's ability to absorb punishment varies widely.

Years ago, when the tobacco industry was assailed for "killing our children," (a feat that fast food is accused of doing today) adult hell-raising committees assaulted factories where cigarettes were turned out. The industry countered by trotting out 80-year old employees who lit up in their presence. The message: Your 19 year old probably died of a congenital problem- not our product."

Food quality whistle blowers are coming up with new terms. When I said "invert sugar" to my periodontist he didn't react. But when I corrected to "empty calories," he smiled and said: "You're not guilty; I can tell."

Americans are addicted to sweet colas and carbonated drinks. "I HATE WATER!" exclaimed an overweight bus tour member when offered some of the bottled stuff. When given the alternative, she drained the can and quickly fell asleep.

I remember my first which was a big event, long remembered. We had a kind, widowed neighbor with a new 1933 Chevrolet. The Big Depression was just getting underway (the family displayed its National Reconstruction Act sticker on the front window), so my sister and I assumed that our friend represented big bucks.

One sultry summer morning, after dad had left for work, Mr. "Smith" collected the three of us in the Chevy and headed for a two lane paved highway, home of America's newest profession, the car hop. The idea of having a gaily-dressed young lady attach a metal tray to the car's door, taking your order while music played from loud speakers, was the hula-hoop of 1933. It was new and, for the average motorist, helped chase the blues.

The car hops wore no skates as they did in California. Concrete and asphalt were too expensive for this brand of private businessman. Nonetheless, the pretty girl served my first soda at age three with a straw, napkin (to insulate the bottle) and great ceremony. It came in a brown ribbed bottle and was known as an Orange Crush.

The brown bottle stuck around until the end of WW II when technology and abundant steel permitted canning. Today's aluminum followed and the "pop" and beer industries settled down to about five nationwide producers each, once Corporate America's "gentlemen's agreements" had been signed.

Modern television's frame-a-second soda selling commercials are highly competitive, expensive and keep many professional actors busy. Computer technology helps keep the target audience addicted, open-mouthed and entertained.

The weight loss hawkers pray for more per capita consumption.

Soda, cola, pop addiction can't be discussed without talking about the scientist who warned against it. Of Dutch-German lineage, Hans Seyle, contributed mostly to behavioral sciences, performing classical population density experiments on the lower mammals and making careful observations of the higher ones, Homo sapiens.

Late in his career, he published many papers on physiology and the internal ailments of modern man, concluding, like his English colleague, Geoffrey Whitehouse, "For internal and neurological health, if it were not available to the cave man, don't eat it!".

His argument: That natural law had built the human body to utilize natural foodstuffs; ingestion of chemical and artificial ingredients added to addict or attract was foolish, untoward and, at times, criminal.

When one thinks on it, their regimen is easy to follow. Dozens of books have been written as guides, and one is included in the bibliography.

---

20. Cooking Anyone?

I had just arrived at age 10 when my maternal grandmother eyed me ruefully one Saturday morning in the kitchen: "You've watched me and your mother long enough… step up to this hot skillet and have at it."

Before me was room temperature butter, hen house eggs, a spatula and bacon from the corner grocery (sans that lawsuit preventative so mandatory today, sodium nitrite). With a butcher knife, kept sharp with a whetstone, I sliced the bacon thin, then used her paring knife to remove the rind.

While the bacon sizzled, I broke two eggs in a small bowl, adding a little seasoning. Soon, the bacon came out to drain on a piece of brown wrapping paper (inexpensive paper towels were 20 years down the pike), and the eggs were carefully introduced to the hot fat. I quickly broke both yolks to let them spread, in case I wanted to make a sandwich. After a minute, I tightly covered the pan and took it off the heat.

"Why did you do that?" my grandmother demanded.

"I saw Emmit Mitchell (our neighbor) do it last month; his turned out real good." After five minutes, I served myself, adding a piece of untoasted bread.

She praised my utility and ability to keep my eyes open while in the kitchen—what she called the "living room." As a cook—the art led to my interest in science—I never looked back.

Later, during married life, the wife and I had no children (probably because of my work with Air Force nuclear weapons) which left us free to visit nearby in-laws and avail ourselves of abundant and outstanding meals on weekends.

My wife was addicted to cigarettes. When a premature death took her, I realized it was time to get back in cooking—seriously. At that time, duty required me to move around the country. Untethered, the ability to pick and choose assignments put me in New York City during 1965.

I lost no time in enrolling with one of the many schools operated by my culinary hero and author of many cookbooks which stressed good food, practicality and economy, James Beard. My class met in downtown Manhattan, not far from CCNY, City College of New York, now known as NYU.

Beard's approach to schooling was simple: One could get into food preparation as deeply as the student wished. Somewhere in the city, he had a school for pastry chefs only... it could be a lifetime profession. But the majority of students came to learn the basics of family and group cooking: how to properly equip a kitchen; how to frugally buy and prepare food without having to pay an arm and a leg for it.

Beard did not teach from the curriculum schedule, but his pep talks about food were inspiring. "The meat and potatoes person is to be pitied and often shunned. The attitude of 'I haven't seen that before; therefore, I won't eat it' is a psychological pitfall common in today's society.

To assure the skeptic that the food being served is wholesome is not enough."

But he was no egoist, often citing the opinions of Julia Child and Elizabeth David, both of whom he knew well.

Our instructors were diversified, some trained by Beard locally, but mostly from Western Europe. After several hours of learning the language of the profession, we finally got down to hands-on training. The first project: How to sharpen knives and cleavers with a butcher's straitening steel; the second: How to chop (shred, dice, mince) vegetables; the third: How to break an egg—one handed.

After eight weeks, 64 hours of supervised cooking chores, I sadly took my leave. A new assignment had arrived and I bade the Big Apple farewell. As a certifying menu, I came up with a Caesar salad (coddle the egg one minute), de-boned oxtails with sauce Béarnaise (simmered in a special beef stock), and a Grand Marnier soufflé (better height in a gas oven).

Chef Beard indicated many of his favorite dishes; I have appended two, guaranteed to generate opinion, curiosity and—approval. New York City, especially as a preteen, always intrigued me from the viewpoint of sports, entertainment and—food. Before fast food, yes, even before the golden arch, the place to satisfy man-sized appetites was the Hebrew delicatessens on the lower east side.[9]

After World War II, they gained in respectability and moved uptown. A major menu item from post Civil War days to the 1960s was the beef tongue. They were like the

Almighty—everywhere! Not only in the delis on made to order sandwiches, but our major meat packers, Armour, Cudahy, Rath, Swift, et al, canned them routinely. Cooked in a court bouillon, skinned and cooled, the grams of fat in a serving (sandwich) take second place to the designer ice creams of today.

Enter color television and secularism. In 2004, less than 12% of the U.S. population cooked once a week from a recipe—that means, scratch. Fast food, with all its obesity through additives which compromise wholesomeness, has taken over.[10]

Food preparation instruction as entertainment, however, continues. The 10 color process is usually at the end of a network's morning "news" session. I observe friends watching these revelations—no one takes notes, nor is any guidance offered on screen.

"I like my food to be cute and pretty," observes one viewer while puffing away. Another wants to know how the anchor person will react when tasting a heart-shaped chicken breast broiled for the first time with the oil of a Chilean sea bass. No one comments on the garnish of chartreuse bamboo.

Having been widowed early in life, I found myself in the company of women quite often. Soon after leaving the Beard school, a Georgia assignment followed and I became reacquainted with Southern values, virtues and traditions.

Word got around that I had spent two undergraduate years at their state university at Athens, so I became accepted into a sea of local cribbage and bridge players.

There was a men's club and sewing circle matriculated into the group and among them there was a great deal of talk about this officer born in the South, but who spoke like a Yankee.

The ring leader and director of events and traffic was one Dolly Hurt who weighed around 80 pounds clad and attacked food as if she had 30 seconds to get it down. Evidently invested with a poor genetic lineage, palsy had set in prematurely and at gatherings she would often stand before me declaring while unable to control the shaking: "James, I want something good (meaning sugar)."

Dolly was a lovely, gentle hostess, reminding me of a skinny Aunt Pittypat of GONE WITH THE WIND. We often talked food and cooking and she knew I had gone to such a school in New York. Without weighing the pros and cons, I presented her and her husband Tolman with a scratch chocolate meringue pie on her birthday.

The unsought results were electric. She telephoned her thanks after inhaling the first slice and cried unabashedly. It took her two days to announce to "the gang" (my term, not hers) that I was gifted in the department and they should collectively gather 'round and avail themselves of what I had to offer. Being the community's Grand Dame, they had little choice.

What had I done? True, I was a trained and dyed in-the-wool teacher, but to instruct a group, mostly women, that had been turning out meals since the reign of Teddy Roosevelt... what had I agreed to?

The base officer's club had a special wing that housed a private party room used mostly for receptions, promotion celebrations and the like. It had a kitchen separated from the main room by a huge folding door. Perfect. Dolly selected a Saturday morning which I reserved, moving in a blackboard and arranging comfortable seating for 25-30.

I knew Southern cooking; therefore, the objective was to cross over into areas they might not be familiar with. After all, the Nation was planning a trip to the moon. New capabilities were upon us.

Early Saturday morning, I moved all tools of the trade from my home to the club kitchen. I brought recipe handouts for the pesto I had made for them to taste. Vegetables to chop, a scarce (at the time) head of Romaine lettuce, as opposed to iceberg, for them to inspect, garlic to peel plus a salad bowl large enough to bathe in.

By 10 o'clock everyone had arrived, poured coffee and settled in. I began with entertainment: Walking among them while using a butcher's steel to sharpen my largest chef's knife… then a small cleaver. On the blackboard I chalked SOLINGEN—the town in Germany that made the world's best koch messers, then and now. Orders for life long tools could be made through Atlanta retailers.

We went through the gamut of tools, everything from a new two-pronged corkscrew to a "stretched wire" cheese and boiled egg slicer. I used colanders and sieves, chopped, diced and shredded vegetables on an easy to clean cutting board.

Passing a box of plastic spoons, I invited them to taste my pint of pesto, that heaven sent, green Italian pasta sauce, easily made in a blender from fresh basil and parsley, garlic, pine nuts, parmesan cheese, virgin olive oil, salt and freshly ground pepper. As the mixture met taste buds, eyebrows were raised. The pepper mill was an oddity to them.

At that time, the steak house style restaurant was at its zenith. When the Civil War ended, the West opened up and beef production zoomed. The steak became America's favorite source of hot, salty fat, but gradually declined to a many faceted burger empire. Aware of the steak syndrome, I didn't get into the many delectable dishes offered by other parts of the steer—including my favorite oxtail entrée first served to White House guests by Jacqueline Kennedy.

I made a fast, simple French dressing in a shaker jar. I trussed a roasting chicken with a pierced lemon in its body cavity, explaining the value of trussing. I showed a long, enameled and covered pot for poaching fish in a court bouillon; the men frowned.

Another handout was a recipe for grape-sized chocolate brandy balls. I passed a cold plate of 25-30 on toothpicks. None came back, and the men smiled.

At this point, I sensed my success score to be 5.0 on a scale of 10; however, with the question/comment period came the dawn. The men present were non-cooks and most attended with wives who, despite my advantage of having Dolly under my spell (unintentionally, of course), proceeded to cancel out and negate all I had proposed.

One by one they invaded the kitchen to demonstrate and make never-ending points:

1) "James (they dared not call me 'Jim'), that dangerous butcher's steel will never be needed in our home; my husband sharpens all my edges. I don't watch him, but in his absence, I call on my son or a friend's husband."

2) "Colanders to drain with? Who needs 'em?" She then proceeded to use a flat pot lid to cover and control the amount of liquid being poured into the sink or another vessel. "I do, however," she continued, "keep a tea strainer for that purpose only."

3) "I don't have a single cutting board in my kitchen. I do shred cabbage for sauerkraut on newspaper, but let me show you how to chop or dice." Selecting a rib of celery, she used a paring knife to section it longitudinally, with the thumb and forefinger routine, sliced the vegetable over a cooking pot.

4) "Your pesto has a different and pleasant taste, but my family wouldn't touch anything over spaghetti (no one used the term "pasta") if it wasn't red and meaty." (James Beard, in his broad knowledge of American behavior, had called the shot on this declaration.)

5) "Your cork screw looks dangerous, too. We've never had one. My brother from Lee County brings scuppernong wine at Christmas, but it's in a screw cap bottle."

Through it all, I pretended to be at a present day cocktail party: smiling and nodding a lot… no opinions or comments. That day, I was the beneficiary, adding to my store of case histories absorbed under the heading of clinical psychology.

Dolly appeared satisfied and flitted among the group behaving as if we had just toured the National Gallery of Art. Months later, during the Holiday Season, I made her a lemon meringue pie.

21. Hygiene

To this day, one of the noblest heroines remains my secondary school history teacher, Eileen McClanahan. Tall, red-haired and in charge, she praised ability, dedication and the United States, often taking it to task if the situation warranted.

In college, her master's degree thesis surfaced infinitesimal facts about Roman Empire justice. Once a month, we got: "How can we revere them today if guilty of dragging their enemies behind chariots—bumpity-bump over the paving stones?"

Her demeanor probably had her rouse Mr. McClanahan each morning, put him in a brace and make him stand (and pass) inspection. We never met him. Still, she was one of the first to challenge unfair consumer mesmerizing by Corporate America.

"Look at my teeth! I still have all of them- no thanks to commercial tooth pastes and powders… which you don't need. Mix equal parts of table salt and baking soda, add a few drops of peppermint flavoring if you wish and you're set for life." It's a regimen I still follow.

She gave a damn about us. She'd put us at the blackboard: "I want you to make a line drawing of the east coast and put in the major cities… louder, Leonard. I can't hear you!" From her, I learned more about projecting than in speech class.

Today, middle schoolers prove to me that Corporate America is indeed in the classroom. Table salt and baking soda? No whiteners! Besides, the expiration date on a dentifrice must be watched closely to insure a fresh supply. Sales per capita are up.

Personal hygiene and public health go hand in hand. If your body is unclean and a danger of contaminating others exists, common sense dictates that steps be taken.

During the 1930s, a great many municipal swimming pools were built under the WPA act. They were managed locally, but Federal guidelines insured that sanitary requirements on hot, summer days were not compromised.

Pool entry was controlled and everyone had to shower before getting into a swim suit. Responsible employees supervised. A foot bath of fungicide to control athlete's foot was mandatory. If a swimmer refused to use it, he or she was asked to leave.

Also mandatory, were tight fitting bathing caps for women. By custom, boys and men wore the hair short, girls long. Head lice, that's correct, head lice and their nits were contained by such a cap, and were consistently found in long hair; hence the hard and fast rule until lifestyles improved.

Or have they? Today, cheap and shallow, vinyl backyard pools are common. Not for swimming, but for cooling off, getting wet. In some of them you'll find youngsters, self-conscious about their obesity, wearing large, dirty T-shirts. Add to that, neighborhood kids in similar attire, uneaten food, two or three dogs plus a hot, humid day and you have the ingredients for a bacterial soup of untoward consequences unless proper adult judgment prevails.

22. Soccer, USA

Soccer is universal "football." You bring up the game in remote—that's a bad choice; nothing anymore is "remote"—non-American parts of the world and, immediately, you're talking a game of the masses; a ball, two marked goals on a level field, willing participants and you're in business.

American football, because of body contact, requires uniforms, training, greater supervision and coaching backed up by funds that assure victory. Although it began as a competitive school sport, it quickly became a professional business with the advent of television.

American soccer, today, is hawked everywhere—from elementary schools onward. To shun it in favor of sports native to the USA is to offend your universal siblings. Not acceptable, says Corporate America; if we are to invest in Globalism… soccer is the wave of the future.

"So, how do we start? How do we slant this approach to young minds?" one CEO wants to know. Obviously, they elect to use their greatest persuader—television commercials. Immediately, delivery men begin making head, knee and foot returns to kids; dogs manage it with a muzzle balance and head return. Joy and entertainment. The seed is planted. Soccer moms and the Sierra Club may take it from there.

So, when a profession league is formed, it probably won't take a name reminiscent of our touted football and basketball icons. Some title which invites a brotherhood of nations will be more appropriate.

My closest brush with death did not come during service in the wars of Korea and Viet Nam… nor in flying the Arctic, nor in Gulf sailing alone, nor in Hurricane Camille, 1969.

Truly, I felt that my "Maker" was at hand during a riot following a huge soccer match. Bucharest, Romania, 1967: When the underdog was beaten by a goal requiring superhuman effort, the crowd should have acknowledged his prowess. Instead, they rioted…the stands coming down, the few police beaten, many, many spectators killed.

As the bent on murder losers bore down on me, I picked up a piece of wood to defend myself, but my light hair and eyes labeled me as a tourist and the mob surged past.

Essentially, the championship game represented the northern Slavs versus the Southern. Serbians, for example, against the Russians. To understand why Eastern Europe citizen hatred runs so deeply, even on the soccer field, one must be a student of the Great War—WW I, the history of which reveals enough to keep a scholar busy for life.

A catfish, Ictalurus furcatus, *from Ohio River Drainage. In the 1920s, catches like this were common in free flowing, clean, meandering rivers.*

In the late 1920s, stream seining was legal and fruitful. Today, due to watershed destruction through development, this stream is a treeless, dry drainage ditch.

Homemade flat bottom boat and locally made "outboard"... The ideal vehicle for river trotline fishing.

PHOTOGRAPHS

In the late 1920s, picture-taking on new two lane paved bridges was legal—and safe.

Twins from a well-to-do south Georgia family, the mid 1940s… before the fast food era. They grew into well developed, successful citizens.

PHOTOGRAPHS

Two family riverbank campsites in the late 1920s. The tent on the right is still in use.

Riverbank campsite. Note the cast iron stove under the "kitchen" fly and the elevated food pantry to discourage night varmints and dogs.

PHOTOGRAPHS

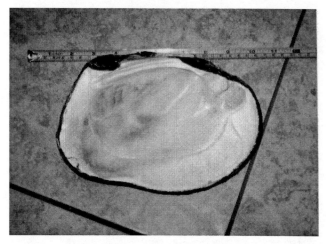

*Valve from a fresh water mussel, Family: Unionidae; harvested from Tennessee River Drainage, c. 1960.
This and related species intolerant of polluted waters, especially runoffs from herbicides and lawn fertilizers.*

August 1922. The author's parents during their first year of courtship. On his twentieth birthday, she has just presented him with a New Testament.

PHOTOGRAPHS

III. THE EARTH

23. Farm Family

Northern Indiana 1939. An Autumnal sunrise on the Bailey farm. A purchase authorized by Zachary Taylor, it has been built up from 80 to 305 acres. It lies approximately 30 miles south of Gary's blast furnaces—a mainstay of the U.S. steel industry.

Bailey and his two sons, 19 and 21 years old, after pre-dawn duties, are feasting on a breakfast of sausage, plate sized pancakes, coffee and milk. They have just taken care of their chief investment: a bull and a dozen pure bred Hereford calves.

The harvest has been good: Bailey has shipped to market 6,000 bushels of potatoes and 155 prime hogs; the calves will soon be auctioned. In the bins and cribs of his barns are 10,000 bushels of corn, wheat and oats. Winter wheat has been planted and fall plowing accomplished.

Mrs. Bailey and her four daughters haven't been idle. The vegetable garden and orchard have yielded 500 quarts of canned fruits and vegetables. The preserve cellar also yields dried beans, hulled walnuts, apples and pumpkins. Her barnyard responsibility sports flocks of chickens, laying hens and geese for memorable Sunday dinners. Her husband, a devout Methodist, makes only sweet cider.

Bailey is a no nonsense ruler; his eldest son will soon be married and live in a house erected on the farm—the tribe will increase. When a sow is slaughtered for meat, the whole family pitches in, scalding, scraping, dressing and quartering for a nearby cold storage facility. When his youngest daughter adopts a young Jersey heifer as her "pet," Bailey explains the bottom line of this attitude toward a marketable commodity. Since dogs and barnyard fowl don't mix, the family doesn't keep man's best friend.

Harvest time success brings leisure time and social gatherings. The piano, a mark of every family with surplus money, is an instrument to be mastered; hence, the eldest daughter is usually the first to be taught and taught to pass on what she has learned. Songs and solos bring the family and neighbors together... not to mention expertise in the local church choir. The work, family and religious ethics are strong.[11]

Today, the Bailey farm, bisected by I-65, Gary to Indianapolis, is a site of community development to accommodate the burgeoning population. The family cemetery plot remains intact (public affairs agents, speaking for developers through the media, are quick to point this out, be they graves of Native American, African American or European Americans—no prejudice, mind you. But no freedom to enlarge it either.)

Percentage of U.S.A. land in farm acreage declined from 60 in 1945 to 45 in 1978. When today's percentage is requested from the USDA, there is no response. Last year's book of facts is mute.

Corporate America has replaced the Baileys with conglomerates that manipulate the soil with gigantic machines while pumping it full of chemicals for eye appealing products harvested by illegal immigrants. The 20% rule on investment return died with parents of "Boomers," and the powers-that-be unabashedly say so on the evening news.

It's an era where dogs rule and the four string guitar replaces the piano… which is a clue to forming your own bottom line.

24. Scratch Biscuits on the River Bank

Before World War II the nation was still largely rural. America's ability to manipulate its topography with earth movers and explosives technology was yet to come. Our population didn't warrant plans for multipurpose dams (power, flood control, recreation) which began to appear during the Roosevelt administration.

Meandering rivers and streams abounded. Nature reigned; the fields teemed with game, aquatic food chains flourished.

Following World War I (The Great War, 1914-1918), America's middle class came into its own, built and sustained by the world's largest and most efficient manufacturing capability.

The post war boom meant better living and more leisure time for all. The wealthy went abroad on the nation's burgeoning steamship line business while the middle class bought box seats at new and improved baseball parks or—enjoyed summer camping/fishing.

The 1920s camping scenario went something like this: Signs proclaiming "Posted... keep out... no trespassing" were non existent. Riverbank farm contacts made during the hunting season usually produced cordial, enduring relationships. "I appreciate the game you've given me," the farmer would declare. "Come back and camp next summer. I'll keep your group in eggs if you keep me in fish."

The unwritten contract was a solemn one: His land was to be respected; ditto, the people and animals living on it. This meant that questionable and irresponsible "friends" were not invited to be part of the vacationing group. Three or four couples appeared to be the optimum size. Beyond eight people, fragmentation could occur.

A week or two before camping time, the men would ask for Saturday off (yes, it was a six-day week) and go first… to select and establish the site. They took precut tongue and groove lumber and 4 by 4s for the tent floors, tools to dig a sealed off privy and cut fire wood, a 100 pound cast iron stove with pipes for a flue, plus a box of cooking utensils. If ice were available within say five miles, a four-door household ice chest accompanied.

It was an era where automobile ownership, prior to the stock market crash of October 1929, was not a problem. Henry Ford saw to it. True, middle class America brought from Willys, Essex and Whippet, but Ford undersold them all, being the first to build early versions of panel and pickup trucks. With advertising that overwhelmed, Henry Ford was certainly the "Budweiser" of the automotive genre.

On day one of their adventure, the couples often went in caravan or perhaps one would arrive on day two or three depending on last minute responsibilities. The women saw to it that ample food for that first day accompanied. No spirits were brought.

The waterproof canvas tents went up first; all had insect netting and some had adjustable "screened" windows. Then canvas cots were unfolded and put inside on the wooden floors along with personal items. Gasoline lanterns were lit and tested before needed. The kitchen area was usually under a canvas tarpaulin stretched between trees; heavy rains were inevitable and prepared for. Someone drove or walked to the farmhouse to announce their arrival and perhaps leave their host a bag of Golden Grain or Bugler if that was what he smoked.

If the campsite had been thoughtfully selected, bathing was no problem. All unaltered, meandering rivers in temperate climates were a series of pools and riffles during low water periods. And if the watershed were intact a rapid rise practically impossible; hence, bathing on a sandbar with smooth cobbles, pebbles and sand underfoot was a pleasure.

Fortunate was the fisherman who camped with a boat, for then he has a chance to take them in abundance… which became no minor point during the Great Depression. Simple boats were wood, homemade and flat-bottomed. The primitive outboards then available were one-cylinder "bangers" with a huge flywheel and wooden two-bladed propeller (If a blade "sheared," you simply hand-carved a replacement.)

Because of abundance, no special license was required to take fish by means of multi-hooked trot lines or seines. (Fresh water commercial fishing came after proliferation of impoundments east of the Rockies, but that's another story.) Armed with a boat and the proper bait, two or three men could take a surprising number of fish on a 20-30 hook line spanning the river, but during hours of darkness, the line had to be checked every two or three hours, Fish in good condition were placed in a sunken "live box" while those dead were cleaned and made ready for the table. If the catch warranted, some campers drove great distances to an ice house that specialized in "cold storage" then returned to run their lines for more.

Depending on the drainage east of the Mississippi, they were catching catfish, bass, drum, paddlefish, even sturgeon in some big rivers. (Bass is seldom caught on a trot line unless it completely swallows the hook and dies immediately.) Baits[*], seined from tributary creeks, were minnows, chubs, crayfish, darters and tadpoles. A prized bait, the fresh water mussel (bi-valve mollusk) took an extra effort. In flowing water three to five feet deep, you felt along a mud or sand bottom with bare feet to find the animal's sharp shell agape. You went down to pry it loose from the substrate. Left in the sun, the valves would part long enough to cut the adductor muscle and remove the animal. Returned to the sun to partly

---

[*] Of the baits listed, minnows (pollution resistant) are now hatchery reared for the sport fishing industry. Crayfish and the true chubs are intolerant of habitat destruction and pollution and have largely disappeared. Mussels, prized for their pink and white nacre (interior valve coating) by the button industry (prior to plastics technology) tolerated impoundments but not pollution. Before WW II, some species reached a length of 12 inches.

decompose, mussel meat on a fishing line became a homing target for fish.

After weeks of broadening experience, the well-fed and exercised campers began to think of dismantling. Truly, no one lost weight. If the men had been up most of the night running lines, the women would let them sleep and awaken to a brunch of scratch biscuits, eggs, and ham (usually salt and smoke cured, supplied by the host). In those days, no one finished dinner without dessert. The portable, insulated oven atop the stove turned out daily flaky crust pies of blackberry, peach or, if someone had a birthday, lemon meringue.

Departure was given the same thoughtful attention as arrival. The objective being to leave the site in the condition found—if not better. The privy was treated with lime, filled in, and marked with stones. The tent floors were stacked, covered by a tarp and topped with evergreen boughs—for next year. Everyone went to say good-bye to the host and his wife who had kids which never bothered the campers. They left the farmer's family with the remainder of his ham, fresh dressed fish and more tobacco than he could use.

Today, camping goes on. Because of the population, it's big business. Everywhere, private land is posted; thus, states are hard pressed to purchase land for state parks and to maintain them with an adequate staff. "Camping" means the parking of an expensive RV (recreational vehicle) alongside its mate. Each has television, bath, air conditioning a complete electric or gas kitchen, computer, bicycles dangling from mounts plus a car in tow which lets the family visit local fast food franchises—those chosen by the kids.

Infrequently, a nylon and aluminum pack tent is pitched by youngsters who have a yen for a night (Benjamin Spock encourages this). But tick scares surfaced by mom limits this behavior. Dad says nothing. "Fishing", usually from a dock jutting into a pond or lake stocked with state bream, consists of rod and reel baited with hatchery reared crickets or worms. Fishery success is measured and reported by a state biologist.

Departure is often spontaneous as dictated by the kids, leaving behind open bags of trash, fishing equipment on the dock and sometimes, the family cat (deliberately?).

25. Adopt a Tarmac

Spring 1950: Dad is taking me for a spin in his new Oldsmobile which came by special order from General Motors. Automatic transmissions were all the rage because they relieved one of the responsibilities of hand, eye and foot coordination required by manual shift. Detroit had geared up for America's indolence.

My father was a pragmatist. He liked to sharpen all senses and keep them that way by frequent use; hence, the special order for the manual shift. I was sitting on his right sipping a bottled Coca-cola.

It was an era before canned colas, steel preceding aluminum. When dating in those days, you could be certain of two events: the soda served you and your date would come in green bottles (Coca-Cola or Seven-Up); she wore white gloves.

But I digress. We were now driving on a two lane, undeveloped road then known as "the country," so when the bottle was empty I nonchalantly tossed it in a grassy ditch.

The car came to a screeching halt. There was no traffic behind us. While staring straight ahead, my father ordered: "Go get it. It doesn't belong there."

Once the bottle was back in the car, nothing was said until we got home. There he explained that the bottle wasn't retrieved because of its value (many stores gave cash for undamaged bottles), but it was a violation of man's (humankind's) "filing system." In other words: "A place for everything and everything in its place." He devoutly felt that world population growth would create unchecked squalor if man didn't observe this rule.

The tenet illustrated is closely allied to the basic ethics of work, family and religion. But the definitions of these ethics are being diluted.

Last month, a family van pulled up next to me at an interstate rest stop. Three youngsters, age's five to ten, opened the sliding doors and raked out 16 pieces (actual count) of fast food cartons, bags and cans on to the tarmac. The front seat adults (mom and dad?) pretended not to notice. But the bottom line and singularly important fact is THEY DID…. and took no action; said nothing. A disposal can was a few feet away!

26. Flood

"Paving over paradise will bring consequences."

(Local editor to me when I wrote the following.)

This year, spectacular rain ruin caused by hurricanes and tropical depressions galore has kept the media busy. Almost to a publisher, the nation's widespread flooding has been attributed to rain volume alone.

To ask the public to buy such a thesis is an appeal to fools. From geologist to forester, earth scientists know what's happening, but you'll not hear or see one interviewed unless carefully edited and the bottom line slanted.

The rain gauge doesn't tell the whole story. First of all, the "countryside" is no longer that of your grandfather or even your father. Comparing aerial or satellite photographs 30 years apart will reveal just how much the land has been developed or denuded.

The European proverb, "To abuse the hill is to abuse the river," can't be ignored. Today, it seems that liberty and life are not enough. We want to live in 12-room homes commanding the heights; our summer quarters built over, as opposed to near, the beach. Henry Beston's beach classic, "The Outermost House," no longer applies. [12]

Factor into development the engineering practices that remove hills and whole watersheds for interstate and mall enlargement, and the damage becomes exponential. Each year, an area the size of Delaware is paved. If rainfall cannot "percolate" into and be held by the soil, it becomes runoff which can quickly turn scenic rivers into drainage ditches or—drown children.

The prime example of paving over paradise is Los Angeles County which began in earnest as WW II ended. The boom demanded quick runoff (Yes, it does rain in southern California), especially south from the San Gabriel Mountains to the sea at Long Beach. By 1950, bare soil was a memory; runoff into the Santa Catalina straits diluted salinity—a big factor in making the California sardine disappear.

Today, in this age of information, our "paving associations" no longer tell us how many square miles are under asphalt and concrete. None, however, is removed—witness the many "out of favor" and abandoned shopping areas that contribute to an increasing danger of FLOOD, a "word of the future" to be reckoned with.

27. Aztlan

In early 1846, with an expansionist president, James Knox Polk, in the White House, the United States was ill prepared for war. The annexation of Texas, regarded as an act of aggression by Mexico, fanned the flames. On our side of the border, the overwhelming of Texans and Americans at the Alamo plus subsequent executions at Goliad, contributed to making the two nations belligerent.

Since the days of New Spain, Mexico had always considered its northern border to be the Nueces River near Corpus Christi. But after Sam Houston's victory at San Jacinto, April 1836, the Mexican president consented to a southern Texas border at the Rio Grande.

After moving into office, Polk lost no time in positioning troops on the river's north bank whereupon they were attacked by Mexican patrols which had crossed over. The president quickly reminded the Congress that "American blood had been shed on American soil" and a declaration of war ensued.

The two-year war, which Mr. Polk oversaw in great detail, was a political and sanguine conflict where a democratic commander-in-chief pressured two Whig generals constantly.

Future president, General "Rough and Ready" Zachary Taylor and General Winfield Scott became household words and sites of their victories such as

Buena Vista and Saltillo became the names of newly incorporated towns, municipal parks and schools.

The capture of Mexico City, by way of Vera Cruz, effectively ended the war. The February 1848 Treaty of Guadalupe Hidalgo fulfilled Polk's dream of sea to sea borders, expanding Texas and acquiring what became the states of California, Nevada, Arizona, New Mexico and parts of Colorado and Wyoming.

Today, Mexican President, Vincente Fox and his nation want that territory back. Given the name AZTLAN by La Raza (the race) the Southwest is under attack, politically, economically and in a clandestine manner.

America's southern border is quite porous, and Corporate America, lobbying Congress for more and more slave labor sees to it that it's kept that way. A recent group of patriots, thousands strong, known as Minutemen, who wish to preserve our sovereignty and heritage, have become Fox's side thorn. He maintains he has 20 million illegal aliens north of the border.

Control of the Congress is La Raza's goal. Current representatives from Hispanic districts have become candid in their tactics of intimidation. Said one in 2004: "Americans know our objectives and are s_____ in their pants." [13]

Fixing the situation is elementary. Relieve our military from its global role of world savior and put troops on the border. Finish a fence from Pacific to Gulf with appropriate monitoring technology. Listen to a military leader who campaigns with: "Give me the power and I will shut it down forever."*

In the quest for AZTLAN, California citizens have suffered most, some fleeing the state after 50 years, witnessing a paradise turn into hell. Those that remain bitch to one another privately about life's quality, but collectively they say nothing.

---

* It would require the mind set of a Dwight Eisenhower who guarded the nation as he would have protected his family against crime and hunger. Such a psyche today, however, would be quite rare among the military. Two terms of military "personnel engineering" by William Jefferson Clinton has seen to it.

28. How Dense Can We Get? *

"I just want everybody to be happy."

(Eighty year-old lady in assisted living when addressing world population.)

In the 1930s, the department of commerce displayed a unique tourist attraction in the nation's capital. A sort of population "odometer," it ticked off the numbers of our growing population. And it got rave reviews. When my father stood before it, his only comment: "We'll never catch India."

After WW II, the boomer growth curve climbed on course and Los Angeles County became Mecca for the returning veteran. We still had a domestic oil supply, a manufacturing base and "Made in USA" became our bumper sticker to the world. Happy days.

But paving over paradise, cheap fuel and irresponsible city fathers led to an unhealthy Los Angeles overcast (smog) and low visibility in St. Louis at high noon.

---

* The question is from a bumper sticker first put out 20 years ago by the Population Institute. Washington based and directed by Dr. Werner Fornos since inception, it publishes a periodic, highly respected newsletter, POPLINE, which pulls no punches addressing the future of Homo sapiens on the planet. Its data, backed up by irrefutable sources, are not quoted by the mainstream press.

Suddenly, we weren't proud of our urban growth. The Department of Commerce "odometer" disappeared.

Today, you can ask any registered voter, country club member, small businessman, "What is our nation's population today?" and they will look puzzled or indifferent (see chapter 1), especially, if they've had a lifelong residence in one state. Ask someone under 30 and you'll probably get: "Don't know, don't care!"

U.S. population is over 300 million, soon to become 500 if our sieve-like borders and immigration policies continue. Immigration is the prime mover; our growth rate, over a given time span, say 25 or 30 years compared to western Europe, is around 36 percent, while they prepare for 5.[14]

The problems of rampant growth are manifold. Witness, Africa after colonial rule ceased. Due to population density and an acute drop in infant mortality, they exist on UN doles and socialized medicine. Witness, New Orleans occupants in the wake of hurricane Katrina—jobless and tied to state and federal doles, they had little choice but to resist evacuation.

The answer to third worlditis is a meaningful job for every head of household—quite difficult when our manufacturing capability is sent south and abroad to Mexico, Central and South America, China, India and Indonesia... all because of corporate avarice and support of globalization.

In 2004, one of every four adult Americans sought a full-time job. It could easily have been one in ten had not these jobs been undersold the applicants to illegal aliens, mostly Mexican.

Adolph Hitler in Mein Kampf: "If you must lie to the people, make it a big one!" Corporate America has done just that in maintaining that illegal aliens take semi-skilled jobs (construction, etc.) that our citizens turn down. If young Americans turn down jobs of this nature, they do so because they are subsidized by the city, county, state or by Aunt Martha or whomever. It's support that can't last; remove the subsidy and they will work.

While very much alive, ABC's Peter Jennings published a pretty, well illustrated work, mostly a subjective coverage of contemporary America. It featured a black two-page map of the United States splashed with white which signified towns and cities—the larger the white areas, the greater population concentration. His bottom line was to zero in on the areas of Black west of the Mississippi, to show the reader that the blight had not yet covered our world—that inoculations could still be tolerated here, here and there... for the present.[15]

It was not unlike the country's first fuel crunch in the 1970s rendered by our dependence on foreign oil. Billboards sprang up along the interstates depicting the planet as one huge gas gauge registering empty with the caption: "What then?" The mainstream media ignored them.

THE EARTH

IV. TOWARD THE UNKNOWN

29. Facts to Face

About the time (c. 1981) "store and lock" facilities appeared on the landscape—they dovetailed with the peaking of American divorces—I began interviewing people for a report that was never published. The typed transcripts are still there, and the file is labeled: THE JOHNNY ROCCO SYNDROME.

A synonym for the syndrome is more/better. Johnny Rocco was a fictional mobster, the archetype Capone, syphilitic and stupid who had one objective in life through murder, counterfeiting and lies—MORE! He enjoyed a year in a Broadway play, hailed for its brutality. Warner Brothers bought the story and produced KEY LARGO in the 1940s.

Today, the syndrome is a way of American life, We have all become Johnny Roccos. The lies and the counterfeiting may be more subtle; however, the glistening eyes and adrenalin pump go into action whenever the key work MORE erupts. Will population density affect our ability to store and protect our loot?

Please permit a short refresher in economics, but we dare not mention it in public schools. A recent two weeks in western Europe turned out to be a study in globalization.

At an old established London hotel, I ordered a single boiled egg in an eggcup to supplement the buffet continental breakfast. The luxury cost me twenty bucks, 10 pounds sterling. The four-fold increase in five years is not due to demand, nor is it because of extra work in the kitchen. The increase smacks of globalization.

When friends and neighbors are told this story, they laugh—which is part of the problem. The once proud yankee dollar is nothing but a slip of paper backed by the credit and faith of the United States treasury. Inflation over the years is normal, but this sudden spurt is scary.

America takes, but doesn't give. It borrows, but doesn't pay back. It buys, but doesn't sell. It imports, but doesn't export (America's largest construction projects are distribution center for imports).

Countries around the world put up with this madness because they are paid in American dollars which they assume have future stability. What will happen when, amid growing discontent at home plus world policing obligations, the dollar descends into oblivion?

As this report approaches the press, a great many unhealthy signs of nation distress and decay prevail. Since its objective is to exhort our citizens to think and act,[*] a list of these signs and events follows. Some are related, others not; hence, the numbers:

---

[*] The late, great Steve Allen is known to Americans primarily as creator of the TONIGHT show. But brilliant, literate and sensitive, he made time to author more than fifty books. One of his last, immensely successful, concerned the layman's lost art of thinking and thus, not acting. For the time of your reading life, consult the bibliography and run, not walk, to the local book shop or library.

1) During April, 2001, many gifted Americans appeared on the C-SPAN television network as a group and presented a program entitled: Population, Immigration and the Environment. They came from far and wide, from government, private foundations, fraternal groups and as individual retirees. The thread that bound them was alarm at rampant, poorly planned growth which the Administration, past and present, appeared to condone. Some of the indisputable facts were gut rending: For example, an area the size of Delaware is paved over annually. Respectfully, their bottom line was to ask the Administration for a "population policy." Today, they're still waiting for a response.

2) For one million dollars: How many registered and qualified candidates ran for the office of President of the United States in 2004? Most state ballots carried only three; some four, if members of Congress were pressured by constituents. To preserve the status quo preferred by corporate America, most were ignored by the mainstream, Orwellian press. For a roster of the candidates and where they stood on the issues, see the appendices. The answer is nine.

3) The Patriot Act has been modified somewhat; still, its message is quite clear: "Surrender your rights and liberties and we will assure a secure existence." Such a proposition paves the way for globalism, a North American Union, an inevitable third world status of doles and socialized medicine... mediocrity.

4) As personnel costs soared (Great Society promises) in the 1980s, corporations took advantage of the computer to get into down sizing, interpreted by many historians as "dumb sizing." The process, coupled with moving manufacturing and service jobs south and overseas, created a profit pattern that corporate America had long sought. Indeed, the process today, in search of complete robotization, has been exacerbated.

5) The great expectation of Boomers has been passed to their children without qualification. Most Americans today, sans transcripts or credentials on the wall, will be the first to admit they know the secrets of life, willing to pontificate from behind a lectern on most any subject. Challenged to do so, they merely pass on TV messages accompanied by frozen smiles and unlimited semaphoring (gestures)—now the union card requisite of that medium.

6) Despite population growth, fewer adults are enrolling in community colleges as opposed to 10 years ago. Tuition is up and adults have access to lottery-funded scholarships only when recent high school graduates are served. Among other reasons cited: Politics. A feeling of hopelessness when once graduated, the vacancy in your field is given to a non-citizen.

7) Concerning rampant growth, a small group of self-appointed, self-anointed "elites" from corporations, unions, religious bodies, universities, entertainment and news media overwhelmingly want (in consort with their personal agendas) high immigration to this nation.

A thinking, drug-free public OVERWHELMINGLY DOES NOT.

8) The nation's abundant, talented actors go unemployed as television sitcoms become prime time cartoons/repeat/cartoons! Producer and network avarice benefit immensely (they are cheaper and mostly free of the human equation), but what does it say about the watcher's mental age?

9) Worldwide, couples are zeroing in on the power of "two incomes and no kids." The TINK syndrome lets them luxuriate in decadent travel and comfort, but it also spells a death knell for the West. Many couples, late in life, make inter-racial adoptions, but case histories reveal disappointments plus dissolution of family ties.

10) If our present national mission of world policeman continues, a return of the draft with all its objections is inevitable. Universal military training would build leadership and character, but such a thesis is not shared by those eligible.

11) With the disappearance of America's manufacturing capability, our once proud and unique middle class has followed—it's gone! What remains is a class that lives from paycheck to pay check; they salt nothing away. As I travel from state to state visiting old haunts, some of the single family homes I knew and visited during the 1940s and 50s remain, not yet fallen to the developer's 'dozer. Generally, the neighborhoods remain clean and unchanged;

however, one anachronism stands out: eight or nine cars (new or in running condition) occupy each lawn... the original one or two car garage probably filled with pets and possessions. In other words, the once one family homes, without adding wings or additions, are occupied by three plus families. Metropolitan areas formerly had "density laws" dictating how many square feet the health department required per family. These statutes, in most cities, have been shrugged away, but neighbors, aware of the squalor and what it brings, continue to complain.

12) Except for a few acres reclaimed from the sea by city planners of coastal towns, no additional land is being formed. Sorry. However, a 133 year old mining claim law (public land statute) is being, at the urging of developer groups, considered by Congress for revision which will open millions of heartland acres for residential development once the nuts and bolts of water and power have ironed out at taxpaper expense. The "open spaces" cited in Peter Jennings', "In Search of America," 2002, may soon be filled with part of the 500 million souls expected for dinner in the year 2050, unless our immigration policy is altered.

13) Defamation of the European American: Television commercial producers have been directed to portray them at a disadvantage; to make them the focus of every stupid product-selling joke and sitcom bottom line imaginable. Drug-free and informed Americans are aware of the trend; still, they say nothing. If races of white, black, yellow and red are to share as USA

beneficiaries, they each must play roles in our divine, televised comedy, <u>period</u>!

14) Under the heading of "extreme makeover," the pursuit of mannequin beauty through surgery, the option of a face transplant has been added recently. As we become robotized, of what value is the façade when the person inside doesn't know that the solid state of water is ice, or that the large country immediately south of our border is Mexico? Surely, some of our wise men/women must feel as Moses did when he came down from Mt. Sinai and saw the golden calf his people had built.

15) In the absence of middle class jobs, some cruel entrepreneurs have found a new way to make a buck. They spread and support the aura of another great lie: That hunger runs rampant in the USA. Corporate America backs them up, sponsoring a spring, rural roundup of donated nonperishable food… "just fill this bag and leave by your mail box; have a nice day!" Acute hunger in the USA? Look around. See any emaciated kids along with the fast food obese ones? Sure, the homeless (This was the first year to see the homeless with kids.) and illegal aliens benefit from the donations, but the common sense answer to hunger, if it exists, is a meaningful job for all citizens. Meanwhile, the food bank president and instigator benefits from federal grants and tax write-offs, not to mention community praise via the mainstream

media… which never cites extreme pilferage at food distribution centers.

16) In our "age of information," disseminating it becomes a problem when a politically correct mantra is in the way. Witness, the invasion of pretty "color women" reporting from the sidelines during NFL games. Women don't play professional football… why should they report it? Add to that, they report in a rhinoid voice against background noise. Male viewers in sports bars ask one another "wha'd she say?"

17) "I pledge allegiance to the United States of America and to… Mexico, El Salvador, Honduras, Columbia and ad infinitum… " Non-citizens are beginning to make dual allegiance declarations without being asked. It's a form of intimidation recommended by La Raza. The Congress should begin to enforce immigration laws and reject such options, then take measures to restrict the practice. But, in light of a mute public, will it?

18) As the population burgeons and natural gas and heating oil prices follow, a full-time jobless public cringes. Power companies react by keeping profit margins intact and professing benevolence. They publish heart-tweaking newsletters imploring financially fit customers to add extra dollars to the monthly bill for the sake of their international siblings. There again, the answer is not embracing socialism, but meaningful jobs—above and beyond Wal-Mart—for all concerned citizens, a position the avarice of corporate American cannot assume.

19) An atheist is suing the government, asking it to remove our national motto, "In God we trust," from the currency. As we perish in an orgy of human rights, he or she will probably win. Already in this report, the judiciary has been indicted; still, the informed citizen should keep a jaundiced eye on it, not because Justice John Roberts is an unusually gifted and interesting guy, but to keep up to speed on rampant change that can spell the end of your world.

20) Recently, the French experienced two weeks of rioting, chaos and the torching of cars and private property. Muslim aliens, mostly there illegally, were working toward a putsch... this was the first installment. The rioters demonstrated against an issue of class—not race. They demanded, in the streets as well as the national assembly, that Frenchmen erase all forms of heritage and tradition tendered them by such nation states as Lombardy and Burgundy, and accept their invasion as a wave of the future. The French populace, mostly drug free, refused and the torching ensued. The government was about to put tanks in the streets when the Muslims backed off, many leaving the country. The USA media was mostly silent and un-opinionated.

Days later, I was present at a local meeting of American Legion officers, and the demonstrations in France were brought up. You could see that minds were working, wheels were turning. I didn't join in the discussion, but the most memorable bit of testimony went something like this: "I served in two wars to protect a nation, the life-style of which is NOT passé... if illegals riot here, lots of veterans will take action. If the Army comes for us, I will be on the ramparts, squeezing off the shots against them. But I question the civilian population! Will they, drugged to the nth degree, rationalize what is happening, as opposed to giving up a gram of comfort for freedom's cause?"

21) Finally, I would be remiss as an earth scientist if I failed to report on a UN-sponsored study that can hardly be shrugged off as sky-is-falling clucking by hysterical Chicken Littles. Four years in the making, the $24 million study assembled by 1,360 scientists from 95 nations spells out graphically (16,000 satellite photos used) the havoc wreaked by pressures on the planet to provide finite resources for its more than 6 billion inhabitants.

The most dire finding of the assessment: Over the past 50 years as world population doubled, human activity depleted 60 percent of the world's grasslands, forests, farmlands, rivers and lakes. A fifth of the world's coral reefs and a third of its mangrove forests have been destroyed in recent decades. A sharp decline in the diversity of animal and plant species now places fully one third of ALL species at risk of extinction.

Close to home examples of ecosystem degradation and abuse include the early 1990s collapse of the Newfoundland cod fishery due to over-fishing, putting tens of thousands of Americans and Canadians out of work. Another cod fishery collapse is imminent. Britain's North Sea staple is moving north due to a slight, but decimating, rise in mean water temperature, making the resource more expensive. Both events were ignored by a mainstream media; still, post tsunami coverage enjoyed the best Nielsen ratings because of its sensationalism/entertainment.

For years, like many Americans, I questioned the United Nation's motives and capabilities. It appeared to take without giving. But, this signal report has turned me around. It makes abundantly clear that the world community must do whatever it takes to preserve its natural capital/resources or face environmental bankruptcy that would challenge all aspects of life on earth.

Allowing grave warnings based on the best available scientific information to go unheeded amounts to inexcusable human folly, with the real possibility of placing Homo sapiens at the top of the 21st century's endangered species list.

QUO VADIS, USA?

APPENDIXES

APPENDIX I

RECIPES

Calf's Head Vinaigrette

If you live in a large city, you can find a butcher to order a calf's head and, using this recipe, gain a reputation for your spécialité de la maison.

Have the butcher split the head longitudinally for you. Remove the brains and tongue; soak the head and tongue in cold water for 2 hours. Clean the brain by removing the membrane and any blood clots. Soak for 2 hours in water acidulated with lemon juice.

Cook the head and tongue separately; the tongue will take a little longer. Put each in a deep kettle with an onion stuck with 2 cloves, a carrot, 1 tablespoon salt and water to cover.

Bring the tongue to a boil, reduce heat, cover and simmer until tender, about 1 ½ hours. Remove from the broth and, when cool enough to handle, skin, trim and slice thinly. Keep warm.

Bring the head to a boil and boil for 5 minutes. Skim off scum, reduce heat, cover and simmer 1 hour or until tender. Remove the pieces and cut into serving portions. Or, with a sharp boning knife, remove meat from the split head and cut it up. The entire meaty portion ears, cheeks and muzzle is edible and delicious. Return meat to the broth to keep warm.

Poach the brains for 15 minutes in salted water flavored with a bay leaf, a few peppercorns and the juice of 1 lemon. Drain.

To serve, arrange the pieces of veal head on a platter around the sliced tongue and brains. Surround with plain, boiled potatoes garnished with chopped parsley. Serve with the following sauce. Serves 6.

Vinaigrette sauce: Make this in proportions of 3 or 4 parts of cold pressed olive oil to 1 part wine vinegar with salt, freshly ground pepper to taste, herbs of your choice and a generous portion of chopped parsley. Garlic is optional.

Philadelphia Pepper Pot

Older generations of Philadelphians can remember this soup being sold piping hot from large milk cans covered with white towels.

4 Tsps butter or margarine
3/4 cup chopped green pepper
1/3 cup chopped celery
1/3 cup sliced onions
3 ½ Tsps flour
5 cups chicken broth crushed red pepper
½ lb. honeycomb tripe, cubed
1 ½ cups cubed potatoes
½ tsp crushed black peppercorns
1 tsp salt
½ cup heavy cream or evap. milk

Pressure cook the tripe at 10 lbs. for 10 minutes, or cover with water, bring to a boil and simmer for 30 minutes. Drain. Melt 3 Tbs. Butter in heavy saucepan. Add green pepper, celery and onions. Stir and cook slowly for 15 minutes. Stir in flour and mix well. Gradually stir in broth (veal stock may be used). Stir in tripe, potatoes, peppercorns and salt. Bring to a boil, cover tightly; simmer one hour. Just before serving, stir in cream and remaining butter. To give the Pepper Pot its distinctive flavor, crushed red pepper and additional crushed black pepper are often added just before serving (6 servings). Serve with beer and rye bread. Try a garnish of crumbled, crisp bacon.

APPENDIX II

2004 PRESIDENTIAL CANDIDATES

18 AMERICAN FREE PRESS • September 20 & 27, 2004

American Free Press: Where the Candidates Stand 2004

	IRAQ WAR	PATRIOT ACT	FREE TRADE	UN	$$ POLICY	TAX FREEDOM
Bush	Supports	Supports	Supports	Supports	Status quo	Favors shifting burden to lower classes
Kerry	Internationalize	Opposed	Supports	Supports	Generally supports status quo	Favors modest reforms
Nader	Would cede control to UN	Opposed	Opposed	Generally supports	Favors greater accountability	Favors shifting from income to commercial taxation
Badnarik	Unconditional Withdrawal	Opposed	In favor; opposed to patronage in its name	Favors immediate withdrawal	Favors immediate abolition of Fed	Opposed to income tax
Peroutka	Withdrawal w/o declaration of war	Opposed	Opposed	Favors immediate withdrawal	Favors immediate abolition of Fed	Unconditionally opposed to income tax
Cobb	Would cede control to the UN	Opposed	Supports WTO legislation of standards	Supports as counterweight to American interests	Unknown	Favors progressive taxation
Brown	Opposed	Opposed	Opposed	Would limit U.S. role	Socialist agenda	Graduated income tax
Parker	Opposed	Opposed	Opposed	Supports UN, but would abolish world court	Unknown	Socialist agenda progressive taxation
Rittenhouse	Opposed	Opposed	Opposed	Withdraw	Cut Spending	Abolish IRS

NOTES

1. *World Almanac*, 1950, p. 299
2. *A Nation of Strangers*, chap. 4
3. *American Free Press*, Aug. 1, 2005
4. *The Death of Common Sense*, III
5. Letter, L, Trella to the author, Apr., 2005
6. *Chattanooga Free Press*, Oct. 2, 2004, editorial page
7. *Masters and Johnson on Sex & Human Loving*, Chap. 13
8. *Stop Poisoning Yourself*, Chap. 9
9. *How to Eat Better for Less Money*, pp. 7-11
10. ABC News ("Good Morning America"), 2004
11. *LIFE*, Nov. 6, 1939, pp. 60-64
12. *The Outermost House*, Chap. 1
13. *The Spotlight* (Weekly), Washington, DC, Dec. 25, 2000.
14. www.numbersUSA.com
15. *In Search of America*, end papers
16. *Death of the West*, Chap. 2

GLOSSARY

ACLU- American Civil Liberties Union

AFB- Air Force Base

AM- Amplitude Modulation

Brown University- Rhode Island's ivy league college whose religious affiliation is Baptist

CAFTA- In 2005, Authorized free trade, unrestricted and tarriffless, for Central America Countries omitted by previous Congressional legislation

CBS- Columbia Broadcasting System

CEO- Chief Executive Officer (General Manager)

CSI- Crime Scene Investigation

FTAA- Statute authorizing free trade for all the Americas, from the south of Chile to Canada

LaRaza- ("The Race") A worldwide organization dedicated to the advancement of and control by Hispanics and Latinos.

MGM- Metro Goldwyn Mayer Studios

MIA- Missing in Action

NAFTA- North American Free Trade Agreement. First of the "trinity" authorized by the Congress to "benefit" the United States, Canada, and Mexico

Narcissism- Abnormal love of self; self worship

NBC- National Broadcasting Company

NOK- Next of Kin

Orwellian- In the spirit of a "Big Brother" society first defined by George Orwell in his novel, "1984"

PCP- Primary Care Physician

POW- Prisoner of War

Riefenstahl, Leni- Award-winning German film director commissioned in the 1930s by Josef Goebbel's to "sell the National Socialist Party (Nazism) to the world." Her end products are globally recognized textbook examples.

Taylor, Zachary- Twelfth president of the U.S. From 1806 until his inauguration in 1849, He was a career army officer and key commanding general in the Mexican War. He often performed civil servant duties such as legalizing/ approving land transfers as in the Indiana deed cited.

T-H-E Syndrome- Teeth, Hair, and Eves surgically or chemically changed to alter the person's facade

USDA- United States Department of Agriculture

WPA- Works Progress Administration

BIBLIOGRAPHY

Books and Periodicals

Allen, Steve.: "DUMBTH," THE LOST ART OF THINKING. Prometheus, New York, 1998.

AMERICAN FREE PRESS (weekly): 645 Pennsylvania Avenue SE, Washington, DC, 20003.

Beard, James.: HOW TO EAT BETTER FOR LESS MONEY. Simon and Schuster, New York, 1954.

Beston, Henry.: THE OUTERMOST HOUSE. Penguin Books, New York, 1976.

Buchanan, Patrick J.: THE DEATH OF THE WEST. St. Martin's, New York, 2002.

Howard, Philip K.: THE DEATH OF COMMON SENSE. Warner Books, New York, 1994.

Jennings, Peter and Brewster, Todd.: IN SEARCH OF AMERICA. Hyperion, New York, 2002.

LIFE, NOVEMBER 6, 1939: Time & Life, Inc., New York.

Masters, William H., et al.: MASTERS AND JOHNSON ON SEX AND HUMAN LOVING. Little Brown and Company, 1986.

New York World Telegram: THE WORLD ALMANAC AND BOOK OF FACTS FOR 1950.

Packard, Vance.: A NATION OF STRANGERS. Pocket Books, New York, 1974.

Spock, Benjamin.: DR. SPOCK's BABY AND CHILD CARE. Simon and Schuster, New York, 1945.

Whitehouse, Geoffrey T.: STOP POISONING YOURSELF! Newman Turner, Ltd., London, 1968.

ACKNOWLEDGMENTS

To me, this page of a work is most important for it gives the writer Carte Blanche to cite people who, along the way, appear in the nick of time to give light to the objective ahead.

Thus, while awash in a geographic area I had vacated 50 years before, fellow writer, pilot and retired Air force officer, Colonel Rube Waddell, briefed me on unknown publication sources. I was overjoyed when, from the civilian sector, banker Joan Watkins and book dealer, Michael Gardner, did the same.

Once contact with the right publisher was made, Hugh Daniel assured me that my memories, interviews and histories would not be untowardly edited or diluted. I am indebted to author representatives Bob and Judy Allen for a pleasant and rapid collaboration. Bob's engineering training and technological expertise quickly filled the gaps since my days of dealing with the Government Printing Office (GPO).

At the risk of being misunderstood, I need to praise my late father, Clarence, for his independent pursuit of unique photographic results, and the common sense to preserve them at proper humidity and temperatures.

Finally, I acknowledge a friend and former commander whose psyche, at times, can be found in this report—the late, great former Air Force Chief of Staff who commented unabashedly during a private interview at the Air War College, March 1977—General Curtis E. LeMay.